BIRTH OF THE INLAND SEA

Fig. 1. The Salton Sea in 2017.

BIRTH OF THE INLAND SEA

HOW THE COLORADO RIVER CREATED THE SALTON SEA

BY

ELLEN LLOYD TROVER

COACHELLA

To the best of the author's knowledge and belief, all of the maps and photographs, except those by the author, are in the public domain. Please see Illustrations: Sources and Notes Thereon for attribution and more information.

Birth of the Inland Sea (text and author's photographs): Copyright © 2018 by History Trove & Ellen Lloyd Trover

All rights reserved. No part of this publication may be reproduced, distributed, or transmitted in any form or by any means without the written permission of the author, except for brief quotations embodied in critical reviews and certain other noncommercial uses permitted by copyright law.

ISBN   978-069219038-8

Library of Congress Control Number: 2018911459

A HISTORY TROVE Publication
P.O. Box 207
Coachella, CA 92236

www.HistoryTrove.com
etrover@gmail.com

CONTENTS

Preface iii

PART I
IRRIGATION AND DISASTER

Before this Sea was Born 1
Construction Begins 13
Mexican Cut 27
The Southern Pacific Becomes Involved 41
Second Break 109

PART II
CONTEMPORARY VIEWS AND REPORTS ON DEVASTATION IN IMPERIAL & COACHELLA VALLEYS

A Spring Sail from Yuma to the Salton Sea 145
Imperial Valley 155
Calexico and Mexicali 183
Southern Pacific Main Line and Other Rail Lines 203
New Liverpool Salt Works 223
Consequences for the Cahuilla 237

Epilogue 247

APPENDIX: Sites in the Twenty-First Century 253
ILLUSTRATIONS: Sources and Notes Thereon 279
BIBLIOGRAPHY 287

PREFACE

There is no doubt, the Salton Sea, the largest lake in California, is dying. It seems that every time I pick up a newspaper or watch the news, there is another article on this vast blue salt water lake bridging the fertile desert of the Imperial and Coachella Valleys.

While researching for a white paper on the Coachella Valley Canal and irrigation system, I found a treasure trove of old resources on the creation of the Salton Sea. Although I grew up (and still live) about 15 miles from the Sea, I had only heard vague references to dirt banks breaking on a canal in Mexico, so I became fascinated by the full story and how prominent it was in the news of the day.

Looking back, there was a lot of finger pointing after the 1905-1907 flooding that created the sea, and a lot of different versions of what happened. Without Charles R. Rockwood of California Development Corporation (CDC), there would have been no one to continually push for an irrigation system from the Colorado River. It is indisputable that CDC lacked the funding to begin building the irrigation project, and George Chaffey used his own resources to start its construction and deliver the first water to the Imperial Valley. Perhaps it is not surprising that two strong men, each with his own ideas, would part ways.

Based on contemporary accounts and photographs, I have tried to write a factual account in Part I; write a brief section on the contemporary consequences in the Imperial and Coachella Valleys in Part II; and present in the Appendix a photo odyssey of some of the sites as they exist today and a modern map of the Torres-Martinez Reservation showing the sections underwater.

PART I
IRRIGATION AND DISASTER

BEFORE THIS SEA WAS BORN

Prehistorically, the Gulf of California extended north through the Imperial and Coachella Valleys; over time geologic shifts and water borne silt changed the topography of the land near the Mexican Border, cutting it off from the Gulf to create the Salton Sink.[1] Subsequently, the Colorado River would change course, on and off creating a vast inland sea, now called Ancient Lake Cahuilla. Around 1580, the last vast lake evaporated.

In the late nineteenth century, the Colorado was still an active river,[2] draining much of the Western US. Springing from watershed high in the snowy Rockies, the "Red River" raced southward and downward, carving the Grand Canyon and other marvelous canyons as it dashed on to the Sea of Cortez. As it approached the Gulf of California, the landscape changed, leaving behind the rock canyons and allowing the river to meander, creating an alluvial delta with the material carried downstream.[3] Smaller overflows of the Colorado River banks continued into the nineteenth century, down the New and Alamo River channels, flowing into the Salton Basin and duly evaporating.

Before the Civil War, the Colorado Desert, to the west of the River crossing at Yuma, Arizona, was a desolate place. Juan Bautistia de Anza's expedition, the first recorded Spanish crossing, traversed it on its way to the coast (1774 and 1775-6). General Kearny and the Army of the West crossed in

---

[1] Also known as the Salton Trough and Salton Basin.

[2] Construction was started on Laguna Dam, the first dam on the Colorado River, in 1905; it was put into service in 1909.

[3] Captain J. A. Mellon, who operated steamboats on the Lower Colorado, estimated the silt extended the delta fan into the Gulf by more than 6 miles over the course of the 40 years prior to 1905. H.T. Cory, *The Imperial Valley and The Salton Sink*, Part IV, (John J. Newbegin, 1915), a reprint of *Irrigation and River Control in the Colorado River Delta*, from Vol. LXXVI, Transactions American Society of Engineers, p. 1214.

1846, followed by the Mormon Battalion in 1847. Some of the Gold Rush Forty-niners and the Butterfield Overland Stage also used this route, known as the Southern Emigrant Trail; but it was a dangerous crossing. Even in the most favorable season, water could be hard, or impossible, to find until parties reached the western mountains.[4]

As early as 1853, geologist William Blake,[5] with the railroad survey, was one of the first to conceive the idea of irrigation of the "Colorado Desert." But the great Reclamation projects of the Twentieth Century were still in its future.

Dr. O.M. Wozencraft[6] is considered the "Father of Imperial Valley" by many, as shortly after the railroad survey, he hired Ebenezer Hadley to survey a route for a gravity-fed canal from the Colorado River to the Colorado Desert. In 1859, the California State Legislature provisionally allocated 3,000,000 acres to him for an irrigation scheme. The Civil War intervened; and although he lobbied for the rest of his life, Congress never approved the allocation.

Everything changed when the Southern Pacific Railroad finished its tracks through the Salton Trough, linking Los Angeles to Yuma in 1877; by 1883, they extended to New Orleans. With expanses of vacant land in the valley, transportation available, and temperate winters, people began to view the area (later known as Imperial Valley) as a potential agricultural paradise.

By the late 1800s, John C. Beatty had formed the Arizona & Sonora Land and Irrigation Company with the purpose of taking Colorado River irrigation to northern Sonora, Mexico. After five months of negotiation, he hired Charles Robinson Rockwood to be Chief Engineer, telling him the investors had two million dollars to back the plan.

---

[4] Perhaps some intrepid souls crossed the sand dunes, but almost all early travelers crossed the Colorado Desert south of the Mexican border, re-entering the US near the site of present day Calexico.

[5] Blake (June 1, 1826 — May 22, 1910) wrote the Introductory Monograph to H.T. Cory's *The Imperial Valley and the Salton Sink*, (John J. Newbegin, 1915).

[6] When he immigrated to California in 1849, Wozencraft (July 26, 1814 — November 22, 1887) crossed the Imperial Valley.

Rockwood's surveys led him to report that the project was infeasible. He then urged Beatty and his investors to explore an alternate project, bringing water to the Colorado Desert. Beatty changed the name of the company to the Colorado River Irrigation Company, relying on Rockwood's advice that what was to be the Imperial Valley had great potential as an agricultural oasis. Due to the physical barriers of the Chocolate and Cargo Muchacho Mountains and the Algodones Dune field west of the River, Rockwood made the fateful decision to build a canal south into Mexico, and use the old Alamo water channel to carry irrigation water about 40 miles west to Sharp's Heading on the US/Mexico Border, and then north via canals into the Imperial Valley. His original plan had been to divert water at Potholes (approximately a mile south of where Laguna Dam was later built). Recognizing the problems of the silt carried by the River, a sluiceway was to be installed near Pilot Knob, just north of the California/Mexico border, and dredges were to be used to remove silt.

There is some debate as to whether Beatty's company[7] ever had substantial financial backing. Whether it did, or if the investors were financially crippled by the Panic of 1893 and the resulting Depression, by 1894, Beatty's company was bankrupt.[8] In 1895, in lieu of unpaid wages, Rockwood received all its assets, including the engineering records, plans and surveys.

In December 1895, A.J. Heber, a former agent for the Kern County Land Company, joined Rockwood in promoting the plan. They formed the California Development Company (CDC), incorporated under the laws of New Jersey on April 4, 1896, with Heber as President and Rockwood as Chief Engineer. Two years later, its wholly owned subsidiary, *La Sociedad de Riego*

---

[7] Rockwood described Beatty as a "Colonel Sellers" type, after the character created by Mark Twain and Charles Dudley Warner in *The Gilded Age*. Col. Sellers was always seeing riches in schemes that never paid off. C.R. Rockwood, "Born of the Desert," *The Second Annual Magazine Edition (The Calexico Chronicle*, May 1909).

[8] On September 11, 1894, *The New York Times* reported an Application for Receivership had been filed, alleging fraud.

3

y Terrenos de la Baja California, Sociedad Anonima[9] ("the Mexican Company"), was formed because Mexico would not allow a US company to operate in that country. The Secretary of the Mexican Company was a Mexican citizen living in Los Angeles.

Throughout the history of his involvement with CDC, Rockwood actively sought investors in the US, Mexico and Europe, but he was unable to find the financial backing to build the original plan from Potholes. So, he modified it to start at Pilot Knob, the last rock formation on the Colorado's journey south. Due to the two problems of the Algodones sand dunes and Pilot Knob to the west, to cut a canal going directly west from the River into California would have been extremely difficult, expensive, and time consuming.

CDC acquired options on 316 acres of patented land along the River in California from Hall Hanlon,[10] and the Mexican company secured an option on 10,000 acres of land in Mexico from General Guillermo Andrade, including the right of way through the Alamo River bed. The new plan was for CDC to divert the water at Pilot Knob, channel it via the Alamo through Mexico, and then to direct most of it back over the border near Calexico, where it would be delivered to mutual water companies. Through three party contracts, CDC would agree to construct, maintain and operate the water system through Mexico in return for receiving the proceeds from selling water to the Imperial Valley. The Mexican Company was to retain the revenue from Mexican users. The mutual water companies would also contract with CDC for construction of delivery canals in the Imperial Valley (Fig. 4).[11]

---

[9] I have found other versions of the name of the Mexican Company: *La Sociedad de Irrigacion y Terrenos de la Baja California,* and *Yrrigacion y Tereranos de la Baja California.* The version cited in the text was that used by H.T. Cory in his reports about the company and the floods.

[10] According to his obituary printed in *The Yuma Sun,* July 19, 1912, Hanlon had operated a ferry across the Colorado from his ranch on the California side.

[11] In Cory's 1906 report to the Southern Pacific on the contracts and finances of CDC, he found that these contracts were not registered with the Mexican government and were not enforceable under that country's laws.

On April 25, 1899, appropriation notices for Colorado River water to be used on US land in the Imperial Valley were given under California State Law. Pilot Knob is the point furthest south on the Colorado where a diversion gate could be built on solid rock; no diversion of water in Mexico was envisioned. In 1903, an application was made to the US War Department for permission to divert water, but the company was told no permission could be given for a diversion already made; however, as long as navigation was not hampered, the Department would take no action.[12]

The separately formed Imperial Land Company[13] sold stock in the mutual water companies to the settlers, enabling them to purchase water. After advertising and other sales expenses were deducted, not enough revenue was paid to CDC to construct the system. By late 1899, Rockwood and Heber had exhausted their personal funds, and Heber resigned from the company. Actually being paid on delivery for water to the farmers in the Imperial and Mexicali Valleys was necessary to fund the project.[14]

---

[12] A 1903 report to the War Department stated there was no reason for the US to take any action to improve the area, since there had been little commerce by ships on the Colorado after the railway opening in 1877.

[13] To untangle and analyze the finances of CDC, Imperial Land Company, and the major participants would be a book in itself. Several people held offices in CDC, the land company, the mutual water districts, and/or the Mexican company, creating confusion.

[14] To give the CDC principals their due, they believed settlement of the Imperial Valley would take place much faster than it did, due in part to problems with the original federal land survey clouding settlers' title, and also to an unfavorable analysis in "Field Operations of the Bureau of Soils, U.S. Department of Agriculture, 1901" and "Soil Survey of the Imperial Area, California (Extending the Survey of 1901), Advanced Sheet of Field Operations of the Bureau of Soils."

Between the Dept. of Agriculture reports, the questions raised about the legality of diverting water from a "navigable" river, and the problems with the government survey lines in the valley, CDC and the Imperial Valley farmers had problems getting credit from banks.

Fig. 2. Professor Blake at Travertine Point in 1908, fifty-three years after his first trip to the Salton Basin.

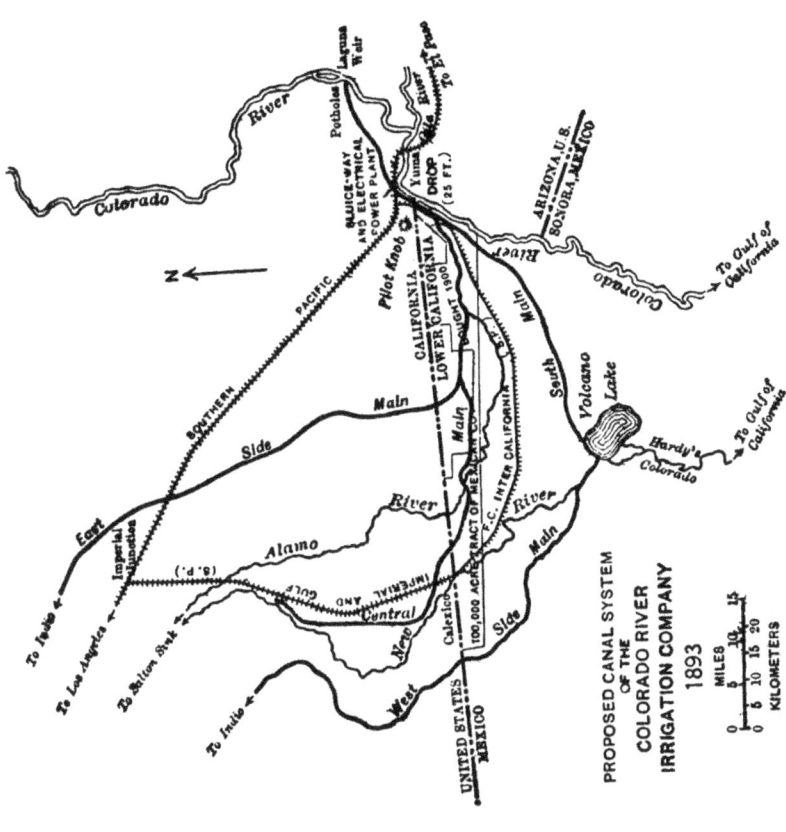

Fig. 3. The plan showing the canal beginning at Potholes and sluiceway at Pilot Knob.

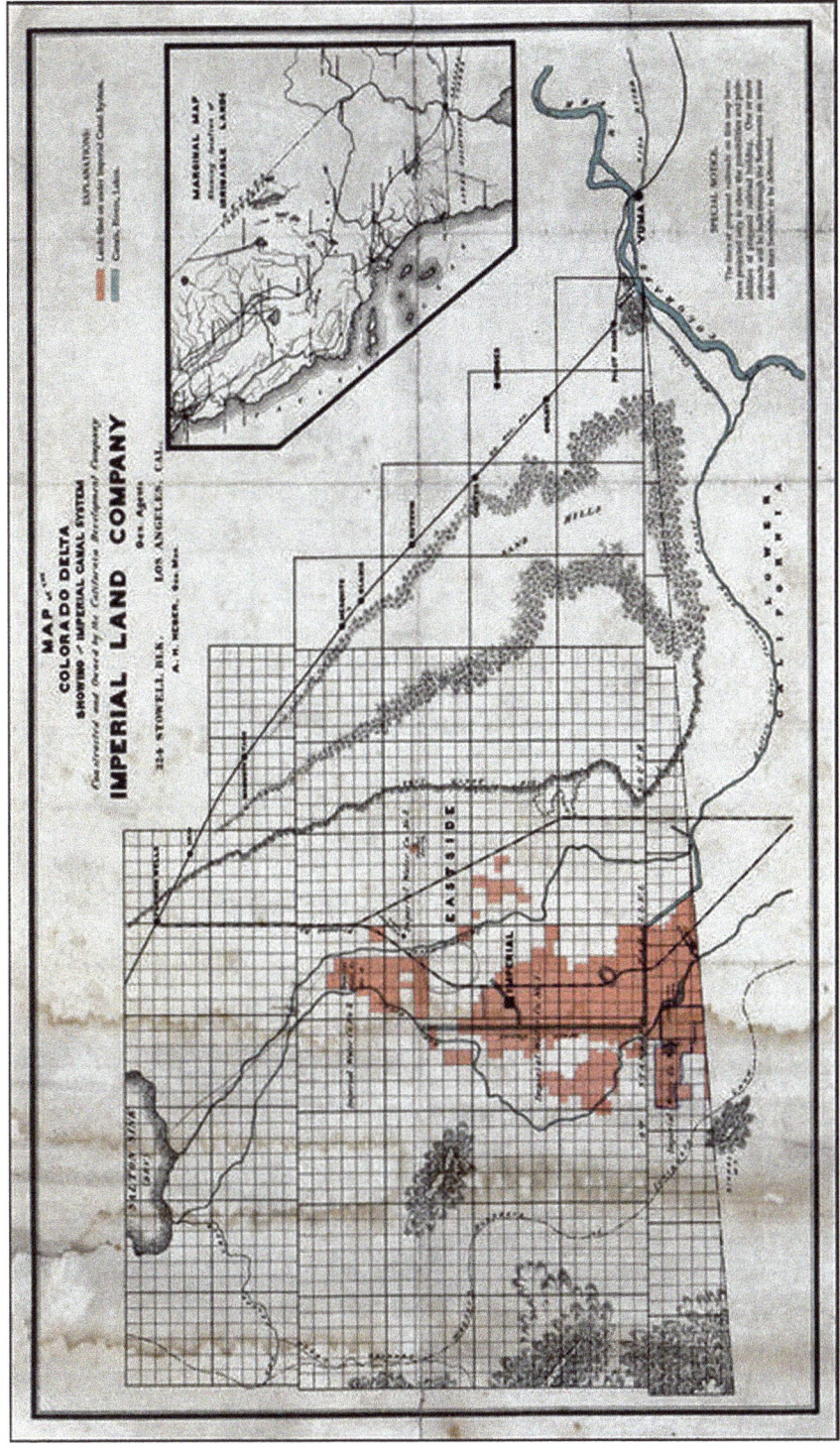

Fig. 4. Promotional map issued by the Imperial Land Company, early 1900s. The curving blue line below the Mexican Border is the new canal/Alamo riverbed.

11

CONSTRUCTION BEGINS

Looking for working capital, Rockwood turned to George Chaffey, who had successfully engineered irrigation projects in southern California and Australia.[15] In April 1900, relying on representations that the company's land options were actually ownership, Chaffey signed a contract[16] to build a canal from Pilot Knob to Sharp's Heading at the Mexico/California Border. He became the major investor, President and Chief Engineer of CDC; at his own request, he had no role in the Imperial Land Company. On Thanksgiving Day, ground was broken for the Imperial Canal. From the wooden Chaffey Headgate at Pilot Knob (on the California side of the river about 500 feet above the Mexican border), a channel was dug south to the Alamo riverbed. The plan was to build a larger, permanent headgate when revenue became available from the sale of water.

At the west end of the Mexican canal, Sharp's Heading, control works

---

[15] George Chaffey (January 28, 1848 — March 1, 1932) and his brother William were successful engineers who essentially created the Etiwanda Colony and Ontario, California; and, he installed the first electric streetlights for the City of Los Angeles. When first approached, Chaffey had not been interested in tackling a project to take water to the Imperial Valley; he and his brother had subsequently accepted an invitation to construct irrigation systems in Victoria and South Australia. William stayed in Australia and eventually became the mayor of Mildura. Their experience with agriculture in Australia gave George confidence that summer temperatures in the Imperial Valley were not prohibitively hot for agriculture.

[16] The representations to him and the terms of the contract were a subject of later dispute, but the fact that Chaffey took control and began construction with his own funds is undisputed. The title issues for the Hanlon and Andrade lands were also cleared while Chaffey was President.

were built: a wood A-frame waste gate in the continuation of the Alamo;[17] a similar gate in the West Side Main Canal; and a combination gate/drop, Sharp's Headgate, to the Central Canal (designed and built by C.N. Perry[18]).

By June 1901, irrigation deliveries to Imperial Valley started. There is some doubt about the reason, but unfortunately, the sill of the Chaffey gate (first intake) was set at 105' above sea level,[19] which was too high to allow water to freely flow into the channel in the low water season (108.2').

---

[17] In an era before telemetry or computerization, diverting the exact amount of water needed to fill irrigation orders was impossible.

[18] Perry also resolved the survey problems in the Imperial Valley by locating the corners of the 1853/54 survey, thus enabling the settlers to perfect title.

[19] Different theories were advanced regarding the placement of the sill: 1) quicksand made it impossible to set the sill lower; 2) the gate needed to be installed quickly to provide water to the farmers; 3) Chaffey was unable, or unwilling, to spend more of his personal funds to meet unforeseen construction cost.

George Wharton James reported evolving information: 1) in the first printing of *The Wonders of the Colorado Desert*, page 507, he places the blame on Chaffey for placing the gate too high; 2) in the second printing of the book, he added an Appendix (page 536), relieving Chaffey of blame as he (Chaffey) purportedly had to complete the first gate quickly due to Spring 1901 flooding, but planned thereafter to install two supplementary gates 5 feet lower before the highwater season of 1902; and, 3) the second view is reiterated by James in *California*, page 305, when he states Chaffey's original plan had been to place the gate at 95' and that Heber had agreed to lower the gate and put in the supplemental gates. George Wharton James, *The Wonders of the Colorado Desert, Vol. II* (Little Brown & Company, 1906) and *California* (The Page Company, 1914).

Chaffey's son, Andrew, later stated there were sand boards on the toe of the gate, which were never utilized. He steadfastly contended that Rockwood, et al, were advised of the sand boards and the need for larger, deeper headgates to be built as soon as money was available. Cory later reported that the Chaffey headgate, although wood, was well built. It did not collapse during the later floods.

Rockwood had wanted it to be set at 100 feet, under the theory that in the low water season, the canal would carry sufficient water to wash the river silt downstream where shallow deposits could be dredged out. In the Spring of 1902, Chaffey left the company, either because CDC failed to deliver promised stock, or because he failed in an attempt to take full control of the company.[20]

Starting in 1901, farming in the Imperial Valley became established, relying on imported water. By winter 1902, the wild, turgid Colorado had deposited so much silt in the canal that the first mile was filled; during the low water seasons of 1902/03 and 1903/04, temporary by-passes were cut around the Chaffey gate, with no gates in the river bank. Upon the approach of summer flood season, these openings were plugged with brush and dirt dams.

Despite continuing dredging by the huge dredge, the *Alpha;* construction of a suction dredge, the *Beta*; running the paddle-wheeler, *Cochran,* up and down the canal with a dragline; and installation of a 60 foot wood A-frame waste gate (February/March 1904), the first 4 miles of the channel filled with silt and vegetation.

The Secretary of the Interior announced that the US Assistant Attorney General had concluded there was no law enabling a US company to carry water through Mexico. In January, CDC lobbied Congress to pass enabling legislation, but on April 8, 1904, Acting Attorney General Hoyt told the House Arid Lands Committee that it would be "unwise" to surrender control of Colorado River water. On December 24, 1904, Dr. C.D. Wolcott, Director of the US Geological Survey (1894-1907), reported to Congress that river water appropriations under state law were not valid.

A. J. Heber, again President of CDC, traveled to Mexico where he obtained a concession from Mexican President Diaz, not only allowing the Mexican Company to operate a canal through Mexican territory, but also to

---

[20] When Chaffey assumed management of CDC, he discovered the land options had expired, and the water filing was about to expire; assets consisted of the work camp and equipment, with liabilities of $1,365,000. When he left, the company had a surplus of $342,687.16.

After the 1905 flooding, Chaffey and Rockwood expressed different versions of why he left. But, by that time, CDC was bankrupt and finger pointing was rampant.

cut an intake below the Border. The Mexican Congress ratified the concession on June 7, 1904.

To meet the farmers' demand, in late summer 1904, a new intake was cut, just south of the Mexican Border (second intake). The company had mounting problems: Congress had not consented to a canal diverting water from a "navigable" river; farmers were filing damage claims due to crop losses;[21] and always underfunded, CDC suffered a loss of credit due to the cloud on its ability to operate a canal in Mexico.

---

[21] All of the claims to this point were settled out of Court, with water or water stock.

Fig. 5. The California Development Co. camp at Intake 1, early 1900s. At the top, right fork of the water channel, is the Chaffey Gate.

Fig. 6. The Chaffey Gate at the first intake, just north of the border with Mexico. Despite what some said later, H.T. Cory stated the wood gate was well built and intact at the time of the floods.

Fig. 7. The Alamo water gate at Sharp's Heading, with 10 foot drop, November 1906.

Fig. 8. Alamo waste gate valves, September 1, 1906. The water not needed to fill irrigation orders was "wasted" through this gate into the Alamo River channel through the Imperial Valley to the Salton Basin.

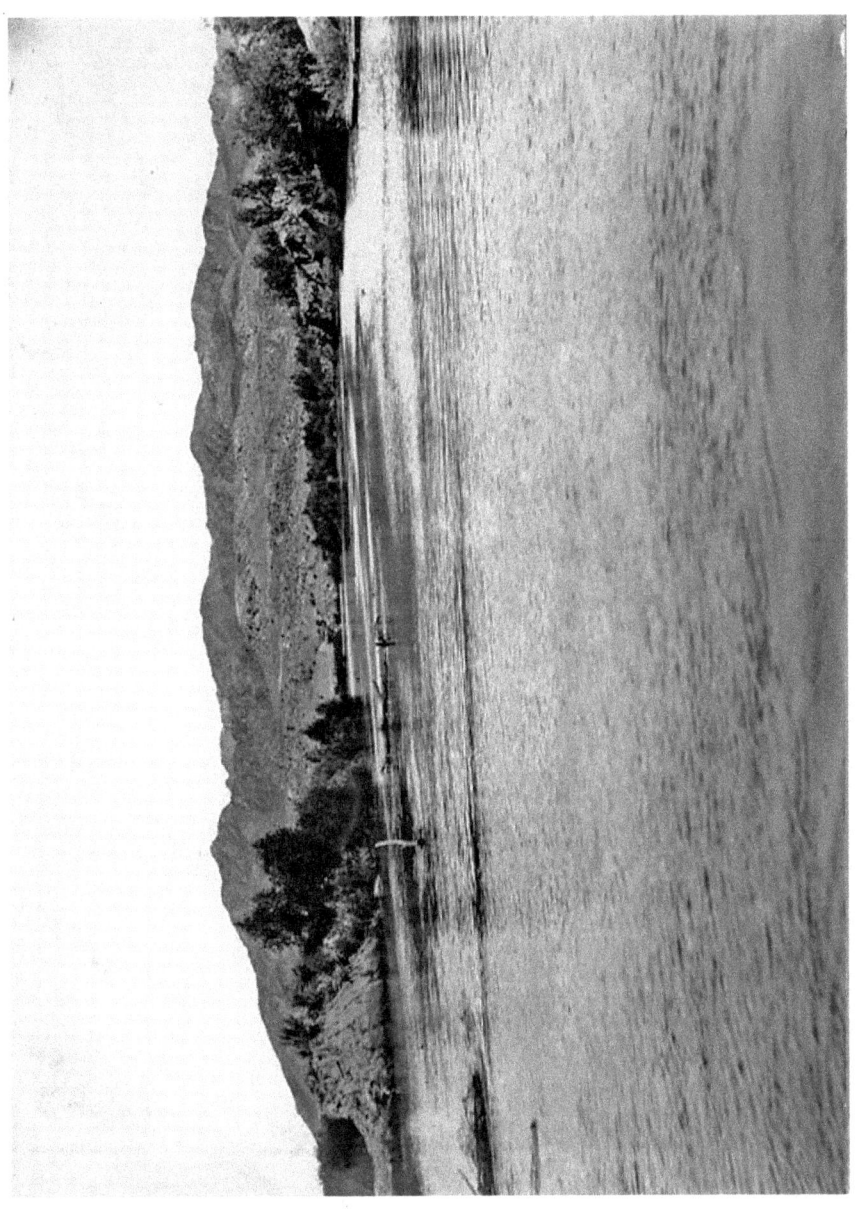

Fig. 9. Second Intake, 1904, cut just below the Mexican Border. The intake, with no headgate, is seen here at high water, with Pilot Knob (USA) in the background.

MEXICAN CUT

Despite CDC's problems, in September/October 1904, Rockwood went forward with a new intake, four miles below the Border; the third intake, or "Mexican Cut" was 50 feet wide and 6 feet deep with a new 3300 foot feeder channel linking it to the Alamo riverbed. In November, plans for the headgate in the Cut were sent to Mexico City for approval.

If Mother Nature had not intervened, all might have been well; but the River was running wild. December 1904, saw unusually high water. From February through April, 1905, five major floods on the Colorado proved more than makeshift dams could control. In April, Captain J.A. Mellon of the steamboat, *Cochran*, proposed CDC scuttle a barge filled with sandbags in the Cut. In hindsight, observers have speculated that the plan could have sealed the Cut and the flooding would have ended; but, at the same time, it would have cut off irrigation water deliveries just as hot weather began.

On May 15, 1905, Harry T. Cory,[22] Assistant to the General Manager for the Southern Pacific Company, was transferred to Associated Harriman Lines in Arizona, as Assistant to the President.

Again C.R. Rockwood was back East, trying to raise funds. At the urging of the farmers of Imperial Water Company No. 1, C.N. Perry made an attempt to dam the water using two rows of pilings with brush and sandbags between them. On Rockwood's return, June 17th, he deemed the water too high and called a halt.[23]

Badly in need of money and finding no buyers for the company,

---

[22] Former Dean of the College of Engineering at the University of Cincinnati and former Dean of the University's College of Law, Cory would become internationally known as the engineer who closed the river break.

[23] Harry T. Cory later thought that a few thousand more sacks of dirt along the upper toe of the dam might have closed the Cut.

CDC borrowed $200,000 from the Southern Pacific Railroad (SP)[24] in June 1905 (Fig. 15).[25] Recognizing the financial management problems of the company, a condition of the loan required CDC place 51% of its stock in trust and to allow SP representatives on the Board of Directors.

---

[24] Also known as ESPEE

[25] Cory, in his 1908 testimony before Congress, said the expectation was that $10,000 would be used to close the break, and $190,000 would be used to pay CDC floating debts and to develop the irrigation system in the Imperial Valley.

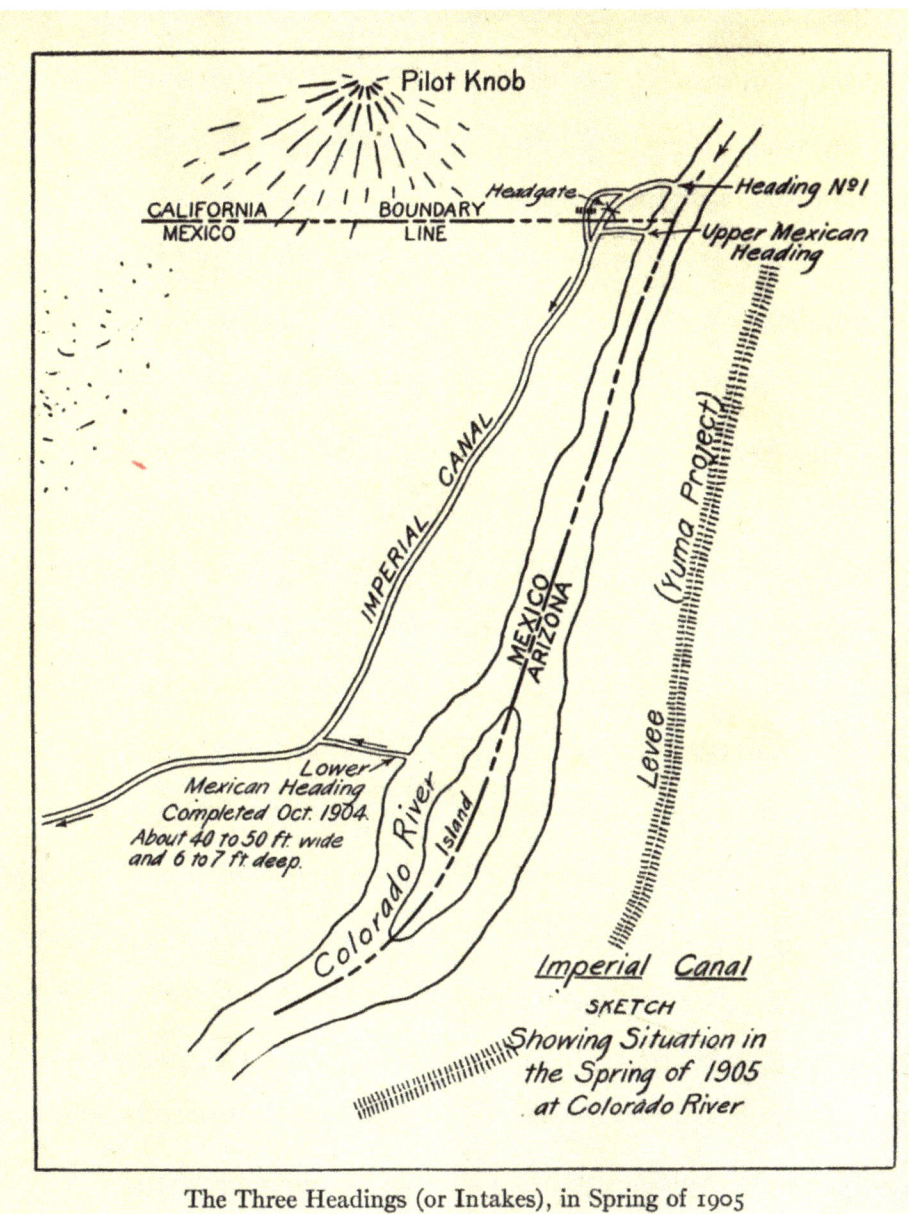

The Three Headings (or Intakes), in Spring of 1905

Fig. 10.

Fig. 11. The junction of the third intake channel (Mexican Cut) and the Alamo/Imperial Canal, June 1, 1905. On the left is the channel dug to carry water from the Colorado River to the canal on the right.

Fig. 12. The *Cochran*, 1900. Prior to the Mexican Cut, the *Cochran* was used to clear the canal by running it up and down the channel with a drag-line. Before a spur railway to the work camps was built, the steamboats, *Cochran*, *Searchlight*, and *St. Vallier*, were the principal way to transport equipment and supplies.

Fig. 13. The *St. Vallier* assisting in the Perry attempt to dam the Mexican Cut with brush mats and pilings, June 1, 1905. By this time, the Cut had doubled in width and depth.

Fig. 14. Remains of Perry Dam, 1905. When Rockwood returned in June 1905, he ordered a halt to the construction of the dam, deeming the water too high. Cory later stated he thought the dam would have been successful with the addition of more sand bags.

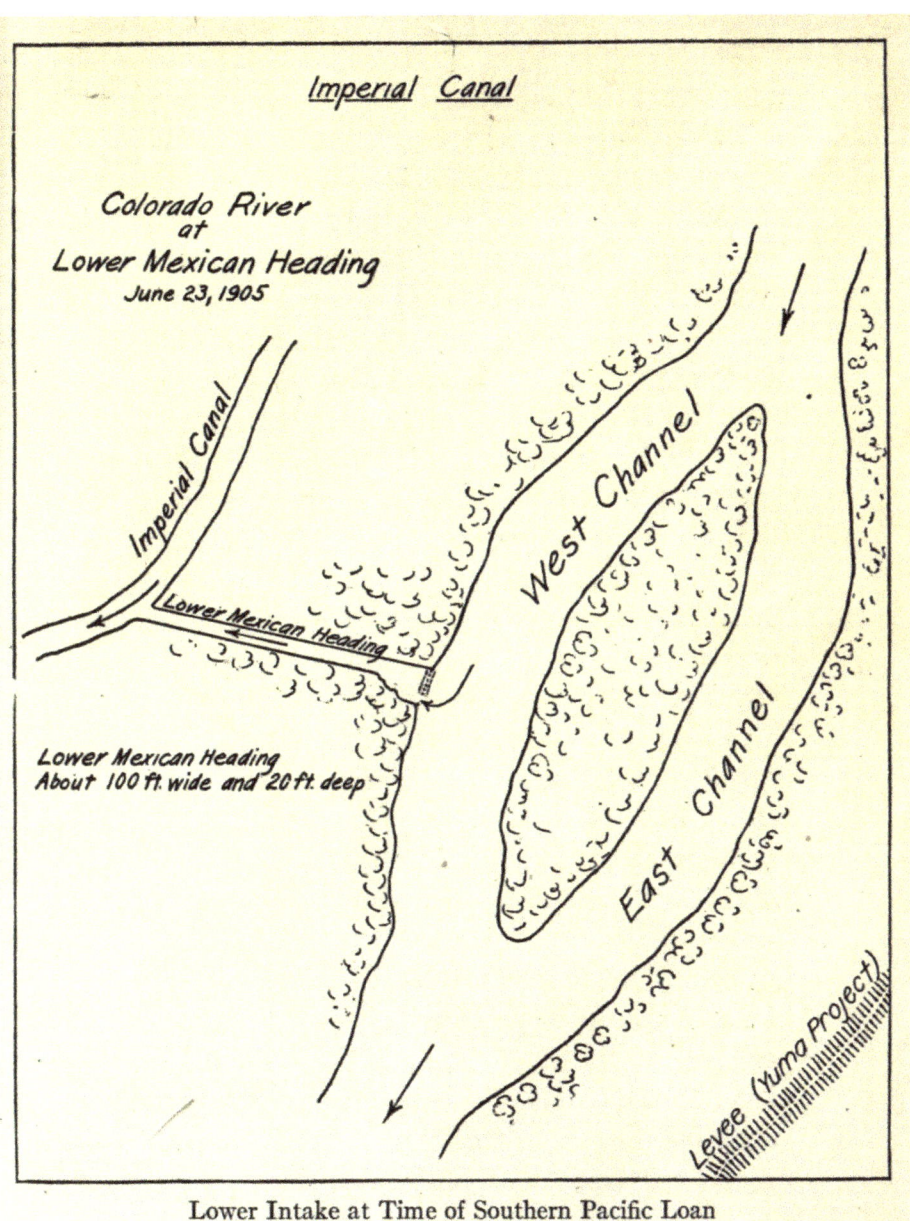

Fig. 15.

THE SOUTHERN PACIFIC RAILROAD BECOMES ACTIVE

As the flood waters began to recede, the banks of the intake collapsed; by late June the Cut had widened to 160 feet (referred to in speech and the press, as "the Crevasse"). On June 20, 1905, the Southern Pacific, the chief creditor of CDC, took temporary financial management, appointing Epes Randolph, President of CDC.

Despite six foot embankments on either side, the railway tracks through the Salton Sink were threatened by the rising waters. Randolph conferred with Rockwood on steps to protect the railroad, and in mid-July, sent Cory to the River to view conditions there. On July 26, 1905, the *Los Angeles Herald* reported the water had reached the tracks.

Trying to find a way to send the River back into its channel to the Gulf, while still supplying the Imperial Valley farmers, Randolph and Rockwood agreed to a two part plan: controlling the River at the Mexican Cut as proposed by Rockwood, and installing a permanent headgate at Hanlon as proposed by consulting engineer James D. Schulyer.

Beginning in July, 1905, Rockwood tried to build a jetty diversion dam from the north edge of the Cut to an island[26] in the Colorado River, to funnel most of the high water to the east fork of the riverbed & thence south past the Cut. By the 15th, one-third of the River's flow had been directed into the channel east of the island, while two-thirds continued to flow into the Cut. By August, a sandbar 2,800 feet long had been formed, leaving a 125 foot opening, but the current was too strong. The dam failed, leaving workers, horses, wagons, provisions, and equipment stranded on "Disaster Island" in the night, to be rescued the next morning.

The water level at the island was 387 feet higher than the bottom of the Salton Sink, approximately 95 miles away by the water course, creating a fall of approximately 4 feet per mile. Due to the meandering nature of the Colorado in the Delta, the fall to the Gulf was approximately 1.25 feet per

---

[26] It was approximately 3000 feet long by 1200 feet wide.

mile; and the bed of the River was rising with the carried silt. Harry T. Cory again visited the Crevasse and work camp on August 1, 1905. Rockwell told him that he was not alarmed as he felt the current was enlarging and deepening the channel which would enable it to carry more water. Cory reported to Randolph that he was seriously worried the situation could become uncontrollable.

By August 9, 1905, the entire Colorado was rushing into the Cut and down the Alamo River/Imperial Canal, headed west and then north to the Salton Trough. Even if the Cut could have been closed, the silt in the first four miles of the canal below the Chaffey gate could not have been cleared fast enough to deliver water to the valley farms.

In early October, the Southern Pacific replaced Rockwood as Chief Engineer with F.S. Edinger, former SP Superintendent of Bridges, who had extensive experience with coffer dams. He began to build a 600 foot barrier dam of piling, brush mattresses and sandbags from the north end of the intake to Disaster Island. By November, the Cut had been dammed. But, Mother Nature wasn't finished; November 29/30, 1905, the Gila River, which enters the Colorado north of Yuma, rose 10 feet in 10 hours, washing out the dam and increasing the flow through the Cut from 12,000 cfs[27] to 115,000 cfs, carrying a large amount of driftwood. The northern part of the island was washed away. Edinger resigned and Rockwood took over again, trying to force most of the water back into the river bed, while also sending irrigation water to the farms (Fig. 22).

After the November flood, Cory made his third trip to the break. Sadly too late, in December, Mexico approved the original plans for a headgate at the site of the Crevasse.

Construction of the permanent concrete headgate began on December 15, 1905; although it was anticipated to take 90 days to construct, it was not finished until June 20, 1906. Hanlon Headgate, built on a rock spur of Pilot Knob, and approximately 1500 feet from the main river channel, was the largest in any US canal, having 11 culverts 10 feet high and 12 feet wide, with 18 inch thick walls, and a pass gate to allow a company launch to enter the canal. The floor of the headgate was set at 98 feet above sea level; at the time, the low-water surface of the river averaged 108 feet. The water was higher on the river side, allowing gravity to feed it into the channel, but

---

[27] cubic feet per second

there would be continuing problems with driftwood and other floating vegetation from the river blocking the openings. An 850 ton dredge, the *Delta*, had been commissioned to be used to clear and enlarge the canal below the headgate.[28] In September, a canal was dug linking the headgate to the Colorado, but the gate was not opened until November 1906, as the channel south to the Alamo had to be cleared of silt and debris.

At the same time, at the Mexican Cut, on December 15th, 1905, Rockwood began pile driving to open a bypass north of the Cut and install a wood headgate[29] in it. The Bypass was designed to carry the entire river flow in "low water" season, leaving the Crevasse dry so a dam could be built. By the end of January 1906, Cory was sent to assist Rockwood with the headgate. The "Rockwood" Headgate was finished on or about April 18th, but the water was too high to divert the River into the Bypass.[30] Rockwood resigned as Chief Engineer on April 19th.[31]

The Southern Pacific through Epes Randolph took total control of CDC, putting Cory in charge as General Manager and Chief Engineer. On April 18th, the great San Francisco earthquake and fires[32] hampered communications with SP headquarters just as seasonal floods were imminent.

---

[28] The delivery of the *Delta* was delayed due to the San Francisco earthquake, as the machinery was being built there while the frame was built in Yuma; the smaller dredge, *Alpha,* was rerouted to clear the canal.

[29] Cory believed it to be the largest wood A-frame flash-board head gate ever built; it was 200 feet wide, 25 feet high, on a floor of 500 anchor piles.

[30] The plan was to divert the low water season flow through the Bypass, build a dam across the break, and join the dam to the southern end of the gate, allowing it to be the future control of the intake.

[31] Rockwood continued to serve as Consulting Engineer until October 1, 1906.

[32] At its own expense, the SP brought over 1600 carloads of relief supplies into San Francisco (a city of approximately 410,000) and transported over 224,000 people out of the City. *1906 Annual Report of the Southern Pacific Company,* pp. 24-26.

Randolph immediately left for San Francisco to confer with E.H. Harriman, President of the Southern Pacific Company. Although CDC had used the full $200,000 loan, Harriman consented to advance another $250,000 to control the River.

In order to both supply water to the farmers and close the lower Mexican Cut, the railway plan continued to be to simultaneously build a permanent steel and concrete headgate at Hanlon Crossing, north of the border, and work on the Bypass and its gate in Mexico.

The upper and lower sections of the Bypass had been started with the dredges, *Alpha* and *Beta* (Fig. 24). Weather reports predicted a heavy summer flood season.

Transportation from Yuma to the Mexican Cut had always been inadequate, relying upon steamboats and barges with shallow drafts. Although willow brush was readily available on the River, equipment and other materials, especially piles and other heavy timber had to be brought by rail to Yuma and then by barge to the work site. Randolph and Cory decided to build a branch rail line from the SP mainline south to the Cut, starting seven miles west of Yuma.[33] Construction on the tracks began on July 1, 1906, crossing the Yuma Indian Reservation without obtaining prior permission.[34] By August 15, the first train was able to cross, carrying materials to the Cut work camp.

By then, flood water had overflowed the Alamo banks south of Sharp's Heading, spreading south and west into the channel of the New River, and thence north to the Salton Trough.[35] Despite the construction of shooflies,[36] the Southern Pacific tracks in the Salton Sink were being critically threatened; continued flooding would soon halt transcontinental rail service at a cost of about a million dollars a month.

Cory believed a piling/brush/sandbag dam would not withstand the

---

[33] Araz Junction.

[34] In light of the emergency situation, permission was granted retroactively.

[35] Cory estimated that in nine months, four times as much dirt as the Panama Canal yardage was washed away by the New and Alamo Rivers.

[36] Temporary by-passes connecting two sections of track

current. Against the advice of numerous engineers,[37] Randolph and Cory decided to build a rock dam across the intake. After doing as much as they could to minimize summer flood damage in the Imperial Valley, operations resumed at the River. Starting work August 6, 1906, when the summer high water had passed, Cory laid 100 foot long brush mattresses reinforced with steel cable across the Cut.[38] It took twenty days, with men working two shifts, to weave and sink the series of three layers of mattresses. While the mattresses were being constructed, parallel trestles were built and rail track laid across the break, which were ready on September 14. Gravel and rock were loaded into "battleships"[39] and flatcars to be dumped from the trestles onto the mattresses.

As the mattresses were being laid in the Crevasse, the level and current of the water in the Bypass rose, enlarging it. Unfortunately, it had a sharp curve and left the intake channel at a sharp angle. When cutting of the bank began, a smaller brush mattress was woven and sunk. When the current scoured the Bypass bed to the level of the gate floor, a barge load of rock was unloaded to protect the bed from being lowered further. On October 3, 1906, there was serious settling of the earth fill in the north abutment to the Rockwood gate; upon excavation, additional small leaks were found indicating weakness. It was decided that the gate would not be safe to use. On October 5, a pile bridge was begun above the gate to connect to the track to the south, with the intent to dump rock from the trestle to fill

---

[37] The consensus was that there were two problems: 1) rock would sink in the silt bottom for an indefinite time unless based on a brush mattress foundation, but that such a foundation would break under the load; and 2) that the current going over the dam as it was built would dislodge the rock.

[38] Brush mattresses were made from bundles of brush, woven together with heavy wire cable. They were laid across the current, by fastening them by steel cables to pilings; as they rapidly filled with silt, they sank under the weight, with the upstream side slightly tilted up. Gravel was laid between each layer; three layers raised the bed by six feet, forcing water into the Bypass.

[39] Battleships were side dumping railcars usually used to dump ballast along new tracks.

the gate, damming the Bypass. The trestle and track were finished on October 11; at 11 am the first train bearing rock started to slowly cross when three bents of the trestle frame failed, wrecking the train.

At 2:30 pm, the gate's mid-section buckled approximately one-third of the way from the south abutment. The larger portion floated until it became lodged about 200 feet away. The wave of water caused by the gate collapse carried drift and debris from the wrecked structure downstream to the railway trestle crossing the Bypass. Although it appeared inevitable that further damage to the Bypass trestles would result, Cory's crews were able to prevent it. Since the water was now entirely flowing through the intake again, it was possible to examine the now dry diversion dam to the Bypass; it showed a "surprisingly small quantity of leakage"[40] which encouraged Cory's belief that a series of rock filled dams could be constructed in the flowing water damming the intake, and relying on the Hanlon Headgate for irrigation water.

The trestles across the Bypass were repaired, and parallel trestles were built across the Crevasse, 30 feet apart. Working day and night, the Bypass was closed on October 27. At Pilot Knob, on November 1, the Hanlon Headgate was opened by blasting the dam blocking the channel from the River to the gate, sending irrigation water down the canal.

By November 4, at the Mexican Cut, the River was completely turned back into its channel using three thousand carloads of rock, gravel and clay, and moving 400,000 cubic yards of dirt (Fig. 40). Built in three sections, the 43 foot high dam consisted of a 400 foot section with a 15° curve at the north end, and then 2,275 feet of tangent. It was known as the Hind Dam after T.J. Hind, Superintendent of the work at the lower heading after June 1, 1906. After a year and a half of efforts to close the break by other means, the current was controlled by a rock fill dam on brush mattress foundations.

After finding it possible to close the break, attention was also focused on construction of levees to prevent the Colorado from overflowing its banks further south. By early December, Shattuck & Desmond, the grading contractors, had completed about 1 ½ miles above and below the dam, 5 more miles were under construction, and another 2 miles had been cleared.

Mid-November, Cory left the River work camp for the first time since June. While off site, he audited the CDC and Mexican company books

---

[40] Cory, *The Imperial Valley and the Salton Sink*, p. 1342.

and prepared a report,[41] showing combined Liabilities exceeded Assets by $2,239,569.98. To meet operating and maintenance costs, 600,000 acre feet of water per year would have to be sold; and the cost of protection against the Colorado overflowing again would fluctuate, but the ten year average would be approximately $100,000 per year.

---

[41] "Report on the Financial Condition of the California Development Company, and its Subsidiary Company, *La Sociedad de Riego y Terrenos de la Baja California, S.A.* on Nov. 1, 1906 by H.T. Cory."

Fig. 16. Abandoned jetty, August 1905. The jetty was designed to build a sand bar which would divert the river into the channel to the east of the island; the current proved too strong and workers were stranded on Disaster Island overnight.

Fig. 17. The dry Colorado River bed below the Cut.

Fig. 18. Workers weaving brush mattresses; those in the foreground are ready to be sunk to create a foundation for the Edinger Dam, November 8, 1905.

Fig. 19. The Edinger Dam under construction, November 15, 1905, two weeks before its failure.

Fig. 20. The wrecked Edinger Dam.

Fig. 21. Remains of Edinger Dam, December 13, 1905.

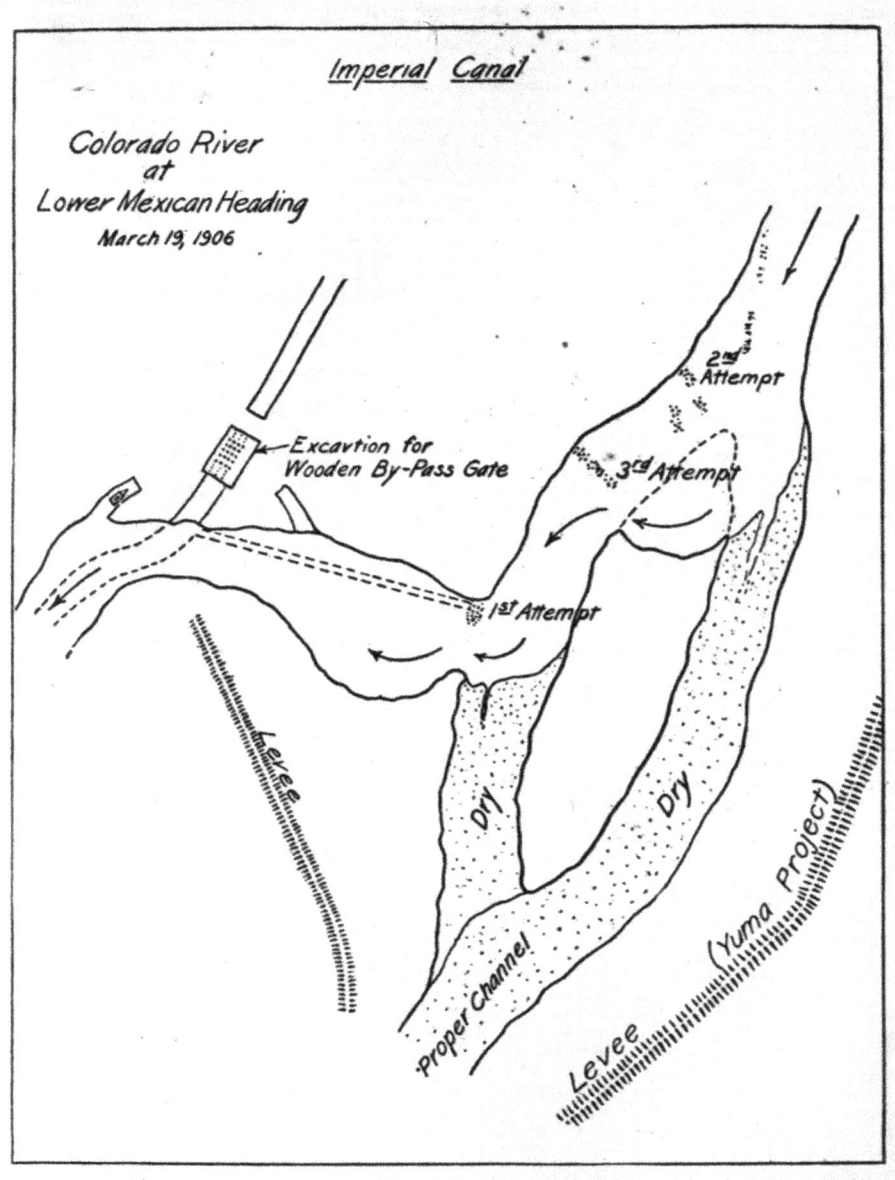

Lower Intake in Spring of 1906 (showing site of Rockwood head-gate and first three attempts to close the break)

Fig. 22.

Fig. 23. *Searchlight* delivering a barge load of provisions.

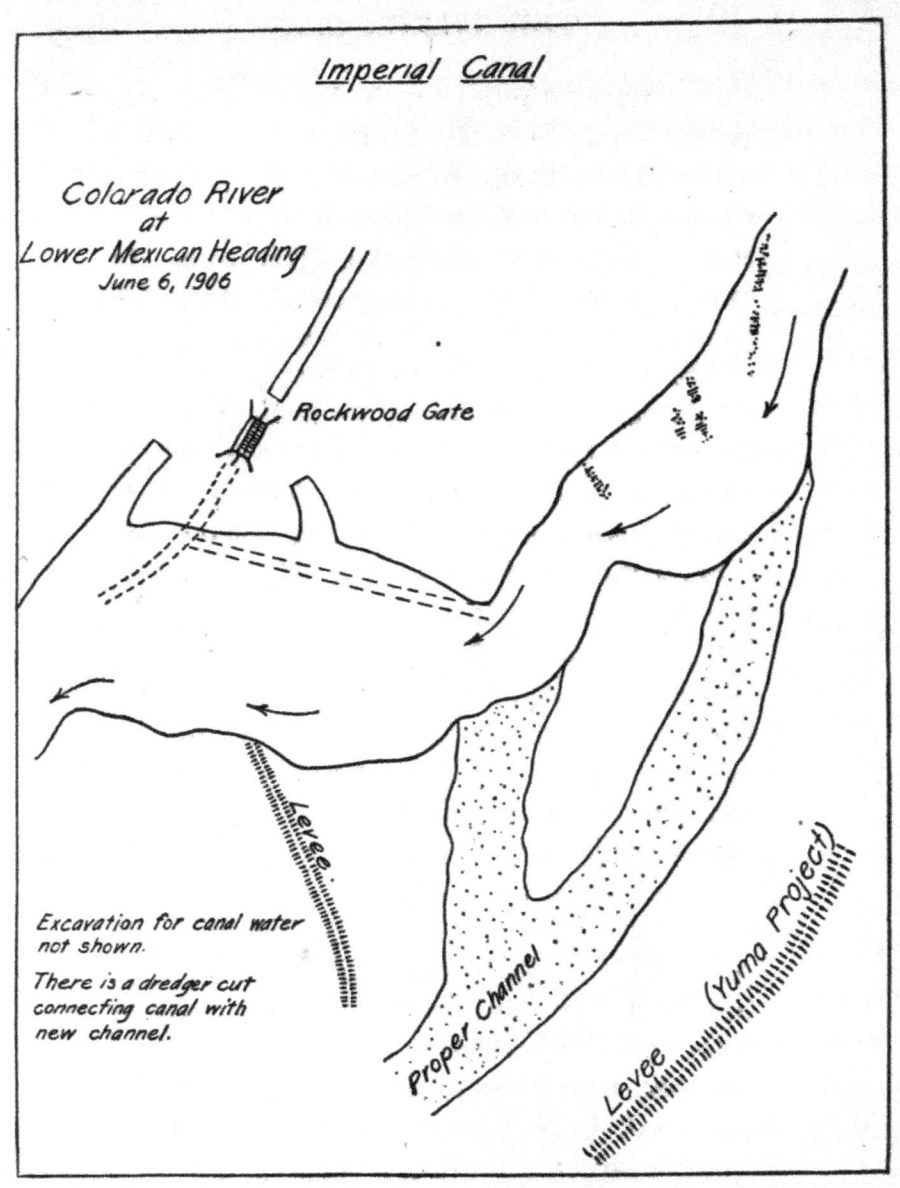

Fig. 24.

Fig. 25. Pilings being driven for the railroad trestles across the Mexican Cut, August 26, 1906.

Fig. 26. Indian workers weaving brush mattresses for trestle foundations.

Fig. 27. Barge ready to lay mattress; photo taken from the north bank of the Mexican Cut, August 26, 1906.

Fig. 28. Brush mattresses being laid; photo taken from the south bank of the Mexican Cut, August 26, 1906.

Fig. 29. Colorado River near the Mexican Cut, August 26, 1906.

Fig. 30. Rockwood Gate in the Bypass, 1906. Behind the gate, two pile drivers can be seen at work in the Bypass, probably working on the trestles; if so, it was taken between October 5 & 10.

Fig. 31. Dry bed of the Imperial/Alamo canal, looking north from the Rockwood Gate, Autumn 1906.

Fig. 32. The morning of October 11, 1906, a train, carrying rock to be dumped in the Bypass at the Rockwood Gate, went off the rails. Fortunately, no one was injured.

Fig. 33. One-third of the Rockwood Gate began to collapse, 2:30 pm, October 11, 1906.

Fig. 34. The collapsed part of the Rockwood Gate floated in the Bypass, October 1906. Part of the work camp can be seen on the bank.

Fig. 35. The damaged trestles and track were rebuilt; by October 17, 1906, battleship cars loaded with rock were dumped to close the Bypass.

Fig. 36. Looking south (downstream) at Imperial/Alamo canal from the site of the Rockwood Gate, Autumn 1906.

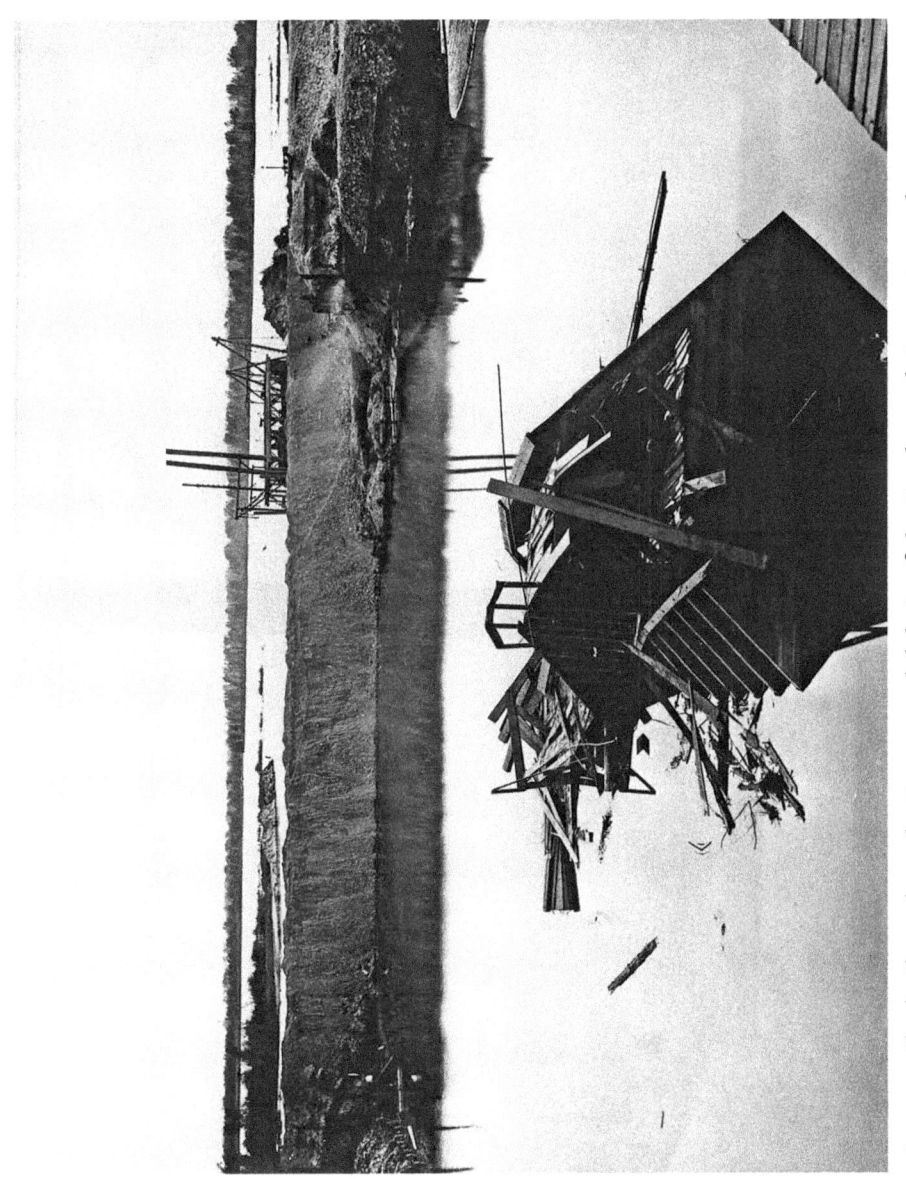

Fig. 37. Dike built to dam the Bypass and debris of the Rockwood Gate, November 13, 1906.

91

Fig. 38. Battleships dumping rock from trestle built over the Mexican Cut, October 20, 1906.

Fig. 39. Boulders being dumped from trestle over Mexican Cut, November 1, 1906.

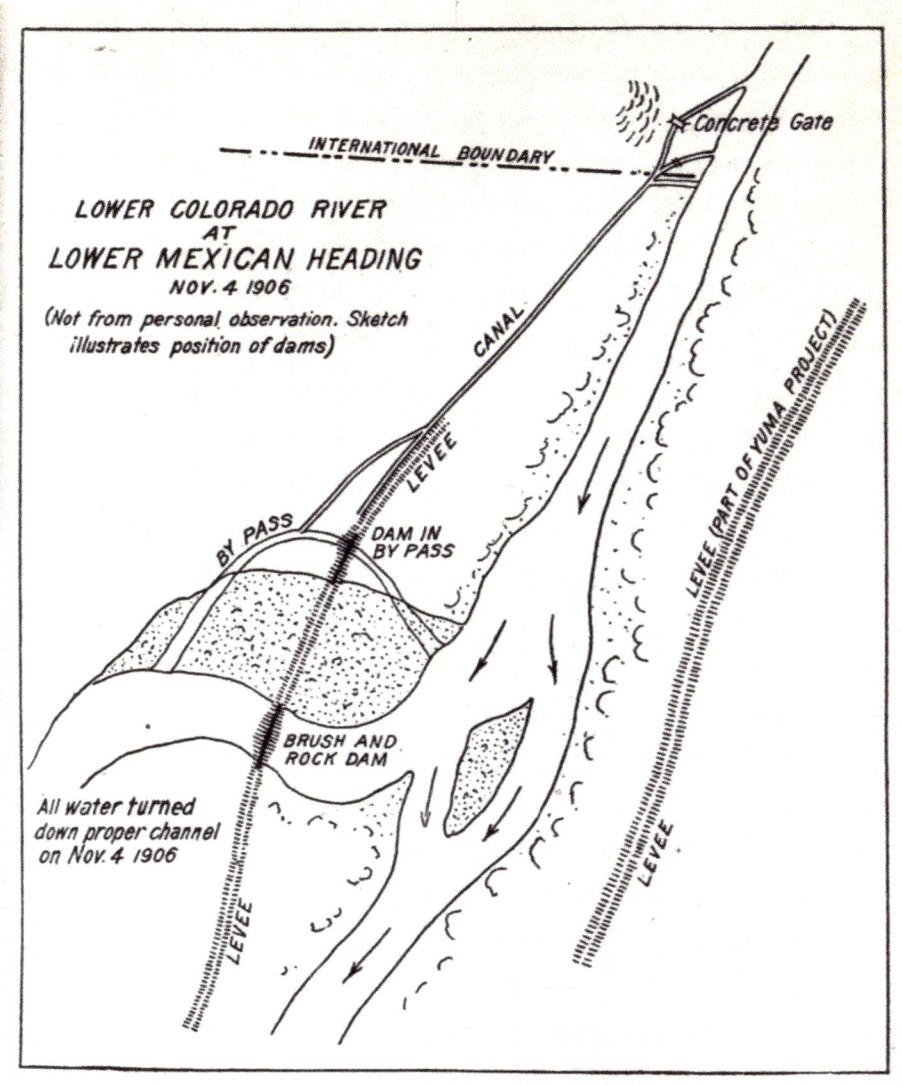

First Closure of Crevasse, Nov. 4, 1906

Fig. 40.

Fig. 41. Hind Dam across the Mexican Cut, November 13, 1906. The water on the left is 14 feet lower than the water in the River, on the right.

Fig. 42. *Searchlight* and workers sealing the Hind Dam with gravel and clay by water jet, November 1906. The level of the water on the left continues to drop.

Fig. 43. View north up the levee, from the Hind Dam, Autumn 1906.

Fig. 44. Work train on protective levee, Autumn 1906.

Fig. 45. Permanent, cement Hanlon Headgate, north of the Mexico Border, 1906.

THE SECOND BREAK

In the last days of November and beginning of December 1906, heavy rains fell in the Gila River watershed above Yuma. On December 7, flood struck the Mexican Cut again. Reaching the lower heading at midnight, the water rose a foot per hour into the early morning.[42] Cory and Hind were in Yuma; learning of the rising water, they returned to the work camp riding a work train, reaching the dam at 5:15 am. The Hind Dam held, but the River had made three serious breaks in the levee about a mile to the south, and about ninety other places had minor incursions. A work crew of 75 had managed to limit the breaks to the three main ones, but by the time Cory and Hind reached the scene, the first break was beyond control. The main breach was rapidly growing, cutting back to approximately 1000 feet from the Hind Dam, and within twenty-four hours the entire Colorado was flowing through the new break (Fig. 46).

The grading outfit, three miles down the River from the break, had been flooded, and the steamer *Searchlight* had been sent to rescue them. The re-diversion of the water into the break was so rapid that the steamboat was left stranded on the suddenly dry riverbed.

It was evident that not only a new dam was necessary, but ten miles of reinforced levee would also be required to prevent future breaks. Neither CDC and the Mexican Company, nor the settlers of the Imperial Valley, were in a financial position to fund damming the new break and building/maintaining the levees. Additionally, the main assets to be protected, in the Imperial and Coachella Valleys, were in the United States, while the necessary work to be done was in Mexico.

E. H. Harriman was faced with a dilemma. The railway had already

---

[42] On November 4, the height of the water was 113 feet above sea level. On December 7, it had fallen to 110 feet; but by 5 am on December 8, it had swelled to 116.4 feet.

spent $1,489,783.82,[43] trying to stop the River. Due to him being president of both the Union Pacific and Southern Pacific railways, he was under investigation by the Interstate Commerce Commission, and only a few weeks before had been publically called an "undesirable citizen" by President Theodore Roosevelt. In an exchange of telegrams, Harriman asked the President to have the 4 year old US Reclamation Service step in. Roosevelt replied Congress was on adjournment, and therefore couldn't authorize the federal service to act; additionally, the break was in Mexican territory, not US. Upon being told it was SP's responsibility to repair the breach, Harriman responded that CDC was not a Southern Pacific business, but rather a debtor to the Southern Pacific. Finally, a compromise was reached where Harriman and the railway would attempt to dam the flow; Reclamation Service engineers would be available for consultation; and the Administration would seek a repayment appropriation from Congress.

Immediately upon Harriman's authorization on December 20, Cory began what would be an epic battle to build a dam across the breach in the levee. Based on what he had learned in closing the first break, he decided to create a rock base for the dam rather than taking the time to have brush mattresses woven. Using five pile drivers, trestles were to be built, topped with rail lines so battleships and flatcars of gravel and rock could be dumped directly into the water.

Between December 20, 1906, and January 27, 1907, parallel railroad trestles were built across the breach, in a curve concave upstream; this was easier said than done, as the raging current ripped out the first three attempts. On the December 28th, when the first trestle collapsed, enough water was diverted back into the riverbed to allow the *Searchlight* to sail north.

As night approached on Sunday, January 27,[44] the first battleship loads of rock began to be dumped. By daylight on the 28th, 145 battleship

---

[43] *1907 Annual Report of the Southern Pacific Company*, p. 25.

[44] I have read secondary accounts that give January 27 as the date the break was closed, based on a statement by a newspaper editor from Indio. However, according to H.T. Cory's reports and other contemporary sources, January 27 is the date the trestles were finished; in his own book on Coachella Valley water, the Indio editor changed the completion date of closing the break to February 10.

loads had been dumped; at the same time, another flood from the Gila River was arriving. On February 10th, at 11 am, the break was closed by the 1200 foot long Clarke Dam, named after C.K. Clarke, Superintendent of the second closing. The flatcar rock on hand, and that en route, as well as gravel and clay, were used between the 10th and 18th to fill the trestle to raise the dam and tracks further as a precaution against future floods.

A year later Cory testified before a U.S. House of Representatives Claims Committee:

> The entire river was coming through this second break. The width was 1,100 feet and the depth varied, but reached a maximum of about 40 feet....Many engineers came out to look at the work... I think without exception they regarded us as being crazy... we went to work and put a trestle across that break and brought in rock at a tremendous rate and dumped it from the trestle.... for three weeks, two divisions of the Southern Pacific system, embracing about 1,200 miles of main line, were practically tied up because of our demands for equipment and facilities. We had a thousand flat cars exclusively in our service, and shipping from Los Angeles' seaport — San Pedro — was practically abandoned for two weeks until we returned a considerable portion of the equipment. It was simply a case of putting rock into that break faster than the river could take it away....in fifteen days after we got the trestle across and dumped the first carload of rock we had the river stopped. In that time I suppose we handled rock faster than it was ever handled before....
>
> We hauled rock from Patagonia, Arizona, 485 miles, over two mountain passes; from Tacna, 60 miles to the east; from three other quarries — one on the Santa Fe, one on the Salt Lake road, and one on the Southern Pacific — all near Colton, about 200 miles to the west, and over the San Gorgonio Pass. However most of the rock was obtained from a quarry just over the international boundary line of the United States which we developed during the first closing.
>
> We brought in about 3,000 flat cars loaded with rock from these immense distances and we put in altogether,

about 80,000 cubic yards of rock in fifteen days. We hauled 8,000 carloads of gravel from a point 40 miles west, Mammoth, and spread over the levees....[45]

After the break was closed, another 956 carloads of clay and 873 carloads of gravel were added to the combined Hind-Clarke Dam. Work, under the supervision of T.J. Hind, continued on the levees for months thereafter.

From the new gate at Hanlon Crossing, on the US side of the Border, south between the canal and the River, the railway repaired and strengthened existing levees and built new ones, reinforced with gravel. A double row of dikes was created, with the west one topped by a railway branch line so equipment and material could be moved in quickly if there were another break.

Two rail lines were laid, one following the west side of the Alamo, while the other crossed the canal over the Hanlon Headgate and then turned south on the levee. In the lower left side of the Tait map (Fig. 57), a spur levee can be seen which was built to prevent any future break from reaching the canal channel. The Inter-California Railroad[46] changed its course to use the Hind-Clarke Dam and the spur levee. In all, 15 miles of track was laid on the main levee, 1 ½ miles on the spur, 5 3/4 miles from Hanlon's Junction to the Mexican Cut, 2.6 miles of sidings and quarry track in the US, and 2.7 miles of sidings and double track atop the Hind-Clarke Dam in Mexico. All of this was left in place. Over the course of 1906 and 1907, the connector channel between the Colorado and the Hanlon Headgate was improved, and the main canal was enlarged and improved.

On June 20, 1907, the blanketing of the levees and dams with gravel was completed. The people of the Imperial Valley waited anxiously for the summer floods, which were large but gradual enough to cut the river channel

---

[45] "Southern Pacific Imperial Valley Claim - Evidence, Statement, and Argument Before the Committee on Claims of the House of Representatives, on House Bill 13997," Sixtieth Congress, First Session (Washington, Government Printing Office, 1908), pp. 11-12.

[46] An extension of service by SP south into Mexico from Calexico and thence east to Yuma.

deeper, washing silt down the delta.[47]

The CDC was broke. In his testimony before the Claims Committee in 1908, Cory's analysis was that under the existing contracts, the company "when the valley is entirely developed and intensely cultivated — that is, after a good many years — will have an income of only about $500,000 a year. The maintenance charges will be at least $150,000 per year, which will leave about $350,000 for interest upon the investment. It will take a good many millions of dollars to complete the irrigation system. The income has never been sufficient to pay operation expenses and now only amounts to about $140,000 a year."[48]

He went on to state he would not accept a gift of CDC stock if it were offered to him.

In his comments on H.T. Cory's report on river control, Elwood Mead[49] stated: "Finally, when it was known that the river was out of control, and the most appalling calamity that ever menaced the State of California was impending, it should not have been left to a bankrupt company and impoverished settlers to cope unaided with this disaster. It was the duty of the State or Nation to take charge,...it was not until this railroad company took charge that we have the first refreshing example of generosity and public spirit. Nothing could be finer than the action of Mr. Harriman...."[50]

There would be more struggles to keep irrigation water flowing to the farms, struggles with the River, struggles in the courts, years of Congressional hearings on repayments, etc.

While the Southern Pacific battled the River, the US Reclamation

---

[47] August 7, 1907, Imperial County was incorporated, severing the area from San Diego County.

[48] "Southern Pacific Imperial Valley Claim - Evidence, Statement and Argument before the Committee on Claims of the House of Representatives," p. 12.

[49] Dr. Elwood Mead (January 16, 1858 - January 26, 1936) was Commissioner of the US Bureau of Reclamation from 1924-1936. Lake Mead behind Hoover Dam was named in his honor in 1936.

[50] H.T. Cory, *The Imperial Valley and The Salton Sink*, p. 1510.

Service was building the first dam on the Colorado, Laguna Dam, 13 miles northeast of Yuma, which was completed in 1909, as part of the Yuma Project bringing irrigation to the Yuma Valley. The Reclamation Era had begun, leading to the major dams on the Colorado.

In July 1911, Imperial Irrigation District, a Special District, was formed; in 1918, another heading was built north of the Hanlon bringing much needed additional water flow and control (Fig. 59). Dredging continued to be necessary.

In 1918, Congress began hearings on plans that would eventually lead to the Boulder Canyon Project. It would be 1940 when the first water was delivered to the Imperial Valley by the "All American Canal," an epic story in itself (Fig. 60).

The Southern Pacific had spent over $3,000,000 on direct river control; between lost revenue and moving main line tracks across the Salton Trough (now the Salton Sea) to higher ground, that amount was doubled. Presidents Roosevelt and Taft asked Congress to compensate the railway for its actions to close the second break, but it was April 1, 1930, when the SP received payment of $1,013,000.[51]

---

[51] *1930 Annual Report of the Southern Pacific Company*, p. 30.
According to the company annual report in 1907, the advance to CDC to close the Crevasse had been $1,489,783.82, and the cost to close the second break was $1,663,136.40, for a total of direct cost on damming the river breaks to $3,152,920.22.

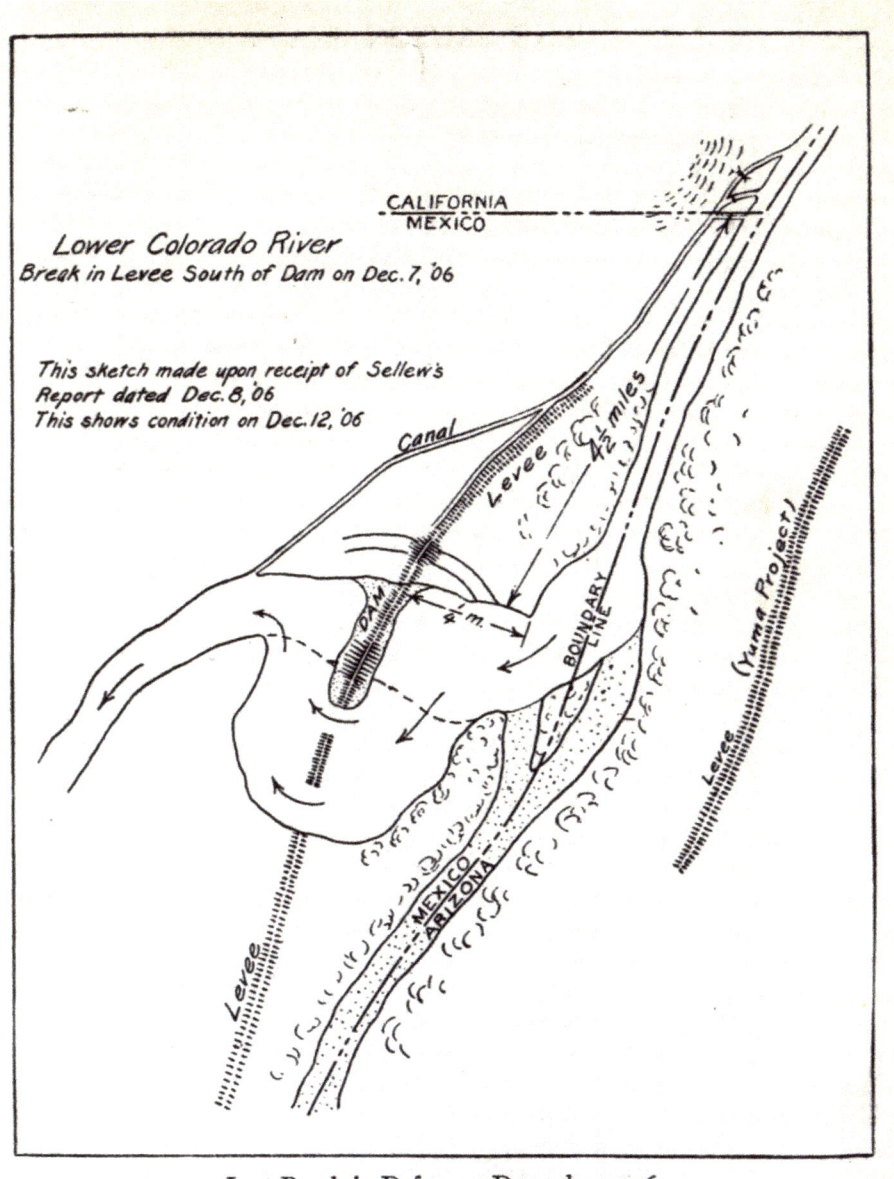

Last Break in Defences, December 1906

Fig. 46.

Fig. 47. The breach in the levee south of the Hind Dam, December 1906.

Fig. 48. Break in levee below Hind Dam, showing river water pouring in, December 1906. I have added a digital pencil line at the end of the levee to make the break more visible.

Fig. 49. The *Searchlight* was stranded on the riverbed, south of the second break, December, 14, 1906.

Fig. 50. Parallel trestles, to be topped with track, were built across the second break, January 20, 1907.

Fig. 51. A general view of the work closing the second break, January 20, 1907.

Fig. 52. Battleships carrying rock on trestles over the second break.

Fig. 53. View looking north at battleships dumping rock into the second break.

Fig. 54. Flatcars loaded with boulders to dump into the breach.

Fig. 55. Unloading boulders into the breach.

Fig. 56. Protective levee, December 1906.

135

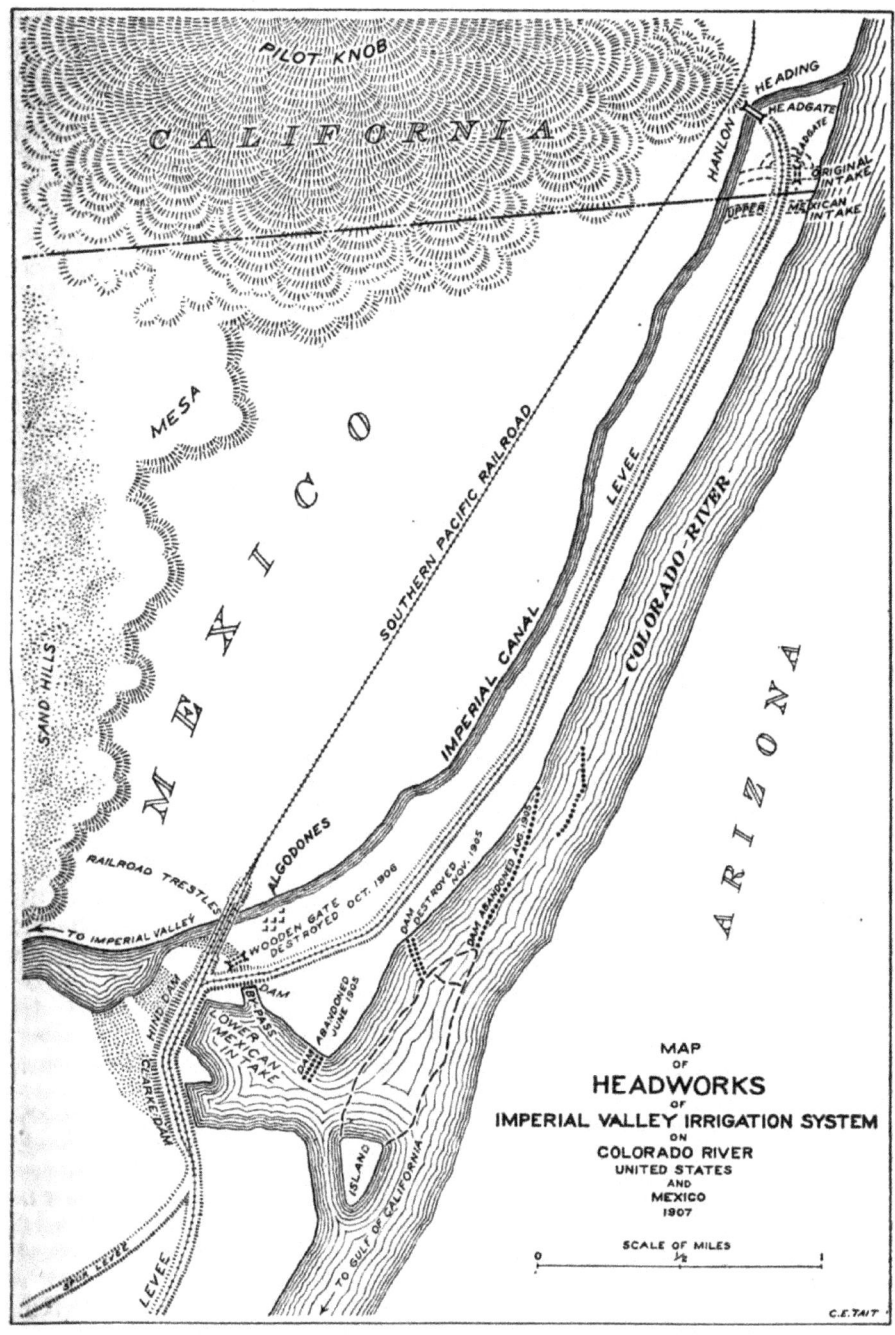

Fig. 57.

Fig. 58. Power scraper at work on Laguna Dam site, December 1906. The first of the Reclamation dams on the Colorado River, it brought irrigation to the Yuma valley.

Fig. 59. 1918 Imperial Irrigation inlet to Imperial Canal. Looking south: on the right is the Imperial Canal with dredges in the distance; on the left is the higher Colorado River.

Fig. 60. The All American Canal, authorized by the Boulder Canyon Project. The canal starts at Imperial Dam and crosses the Algodones dunes, staying inside the US Border to deliver irrigation water to Imperial Valley (delivery began in 1940).

PART II
CONTEMPORARY VIEWS AND REPORTS ON DEVASTATION IN IMPERIAL & COACHELLA VALLEYS

A SPRING SAIL FROM YUMA TO THE SALTON SEA

A contemporary view of what was happening on the Alamo River between the Colorado and the Sea, can be found in Chapter XXXV of George Wharton James' *The Wonders of the Colorado Desert*, published in December 1906. Leaving Yuma on March 8, 1906, the explorer/writer/photographer George Wharton James and five companions[52] set forth to be the first to sail from Yuma to the Salton Sea via the Alamo River.

The first day was easy sailing with the Colorado River current. On reaching the site of their first camp, the artist among them, Judson, set up his easel to paint the glory of sunset on the Colorado River.

The next day, after examining the concrete headgate being built at Hanlon, they sailed to the site of the Rockwood gate. About a mile further south, they reached the work camp.

Two Indians joined them when the party[53] left the work camp at the

---

[52] His account gives only last names; with the exception of " Grippie" Gripton of New York, whose first name is still unknown to me, they were:

Louis Francis "Brownie" Brown: business manager for lecturer, Burton Holmes;

William L. Judson, Dean of the Fine Arts Department, University of Southern California;

Frank T. Lea, missionary to the Yuma Indians (the Fort Yuma Quechan Indians);

Lea "Van" Van Anderson, assistant to James and cartographer for the expedition.

[53] Although his book states the "six" left the work camp at the intake, there were no later references to Judson, even when James named each traveler and where they slept on the boats on the night they had to spend in the mesquite forest. Nor, was Judson named when three (Gripton,

Mexican Cut. James's first hand account of their harrowing adventure down the Alamo is fascinating reading.

Since the Colorado had turned its full flow into the Cut, the first ten miles on the now 1000 foot wide Alamo "canal" were rapid but smooth sailing. Then for the next ten miles, the water spread out into a thorny mesquite forest where the current diminished and a channel was hard to locate; the men ended up sleeping in the boats, and during the day cutting the submerged trees below water to create a passage for the boats.[54]

Eventually, the water returned to a channel and the next night was spent on the bank in Mexico. The following day they sighted multitudes of sea birds, especially pelicans. By afternoon, they reached Sharp's Heading on the Mexican border. From there, the water was funneled through gates into the canals to the Imperial Valley farms, and via a waste gate into the Alamo River channel to the Salton Sea.

Between Sharp's and the Sea, there were approximately fifty miles of the Alamo River and a drop in altitude of 300 feet, causing multitudes of rapids. One of their three boats was left behind.

At Holtville, Gripton, Brown and Lea departed, leaving James and Van Anderson, with their Indian guide, to run the remaining, over fifty, rapids. Along the way, the "river" of water undercut the banks, sending large avalanches of earth falling; luckily their boats were not swamped.

Finally, the remaining three men reached the Salton Trough, where the wind whipped up, causing waves and driving them off course. Their boat took on so much water that they decided to abandon crossing the Salton Sea

---

Brown and Lea) left the group at Holtville; he specifically said only he and Van Anderson went on with their Indian guide. I believe Professor Judson left the group at the work camp.

[54] James' description of their progress: "Many a time we had to resort to machete, hatchet, or axe and literally chop our way through. Then, as the many divisions and diversions of the current reduced the flow of water, we ran onto sand-bars in these mesquites and for hours at a time had to wade in the water, up to our middles, often sinking in the quicksands up to our knees and higher, lifting, pushing, pulling, straining to get our boats along while the mesquite thorns got in their work." George Wharton James, *The Wonders of the Colorado Desert, Vol. II*, p. 492.

and cached their stores on a butte above sea level. With much struggle, carrying their cameras, water and food, they walked the last 18 miles to the railway at Imperial Junction.[55]

---

[55] Renamed Niland in 1914.

Fig. 61. Professor Judson set up his easel on the bank of the Colorado, March 1906.

Fig. 62. James boats on the Alamo River in the Imperial Valley, two days from the Salton Sea, March 1906.

Fig. 63. Pelicans in the air and on an island in the Salton Sea.

IMPERIAL VALLEY

When the water exceeded the Alamo Channel capacity, it overflowed, seeking another route. The two primary conduits between the Alamo and the New Rivers were the Beltran and Garza Sloughs in Mexico.

As the Colorado water reached the Salton Sink, it began cutting deeper channels in the earth, leading to undercutting the banks.[56] Cataracts began advancing upstream. On opposite sides of the town of Imperial, the New and Alamo Rivers cut gorges 60-80 feet deep.

On June 4, 1906, the New River cut the main canal of Mutual Water District 2, just above Five Headings.[57]

In August the Alamo cataract passed Holtville, causing the power plant to be temporarily shut down.[58]

Due to the loss of flumes carrying irrigation over the old water beds, from the summer of 1906 through January of 1907, Districts 6 and 8 received no water, causing 30,000 acres of land to be abandoned, of which 12,000 had been under cultivation. There was increasing fear that if the New River cataract reached the junction of the two rivers, the entire Colorado would be diverted away from the Alamo course to Sharp's Heading, cutting off all irrigation to the valley.

---

[56] After the ancient river had built an alluvial delta that caused the water to flow to the Gulf, overflows of the Colorado had been more gradual, unlike the raging currents of 1906.

[57] At "Five Headings," the main Imperial Canal was divided by five gates to: 1) an extension of the main canal north to District No. 4; 2) a waste gate to the New River channel; and 3-5) three gates to laterals of District No. 1.

[58] Eventually, a new power plant was built at a lower elevation to take advantage of the fall into the gorge.

Imperial Valley and Baja California lands were not the only areas threatened. In an address to the National Geographic Society on November 23, 1906, Arthur P. Davis stated that had the railroad not stopped the River, "This cutting would be continued until the 200 odd feet of excess fall in the channel had been distributed up the Colorado River, eventually, perhaps as far as The Needles. It certainly would have cut a deep channel up to Parker — so deep that it would probably have been entirely impracticable to dam and divert the Colorado River at any point below Bill Williams Fork,..."[59]

The damage to the Imperial Valley was not without a benefit. When the intake was closed in 1907, the popular belief was the Salton Sea would evaporate in 15/20 years, as it had from past overflows. However, the water brought to the Imperial Valley via the Imperial Canal, and later the All-American Canal, had to drain somewhere. At its peak water consumption, the Imperial Valley used approximately 3 million acre feet of water per year.[60]

The elevation of Calexico is approximately three feet, whereas the bottom of the sea is 278 feet below sea level.[61] The scouring of the Alamo and New River channels by the flood waters made them natural drains, headed north to the Sea that has no outlet.

---

[59] Assistant Chief Engineer, U.S. Reclamation Service, printed in "The New Inland Sea," *National Geographic Magazine*, January 1907, p. 42.

[60] Silt and salt historically destroyed irrigation systems, leaving the ditches clogged and the land alkaline. The drainage into the Salton Sea allowed the drain water to carry both away.

But be careful what you wish for. The benefit of having a sink for agricultural water has also led to the problems of over a century of sediments carried to the Sea, significantly contributing to the current problems of the Sea.

[61] *1907 Annual Report, Southern Pacific Company*, p. 25.

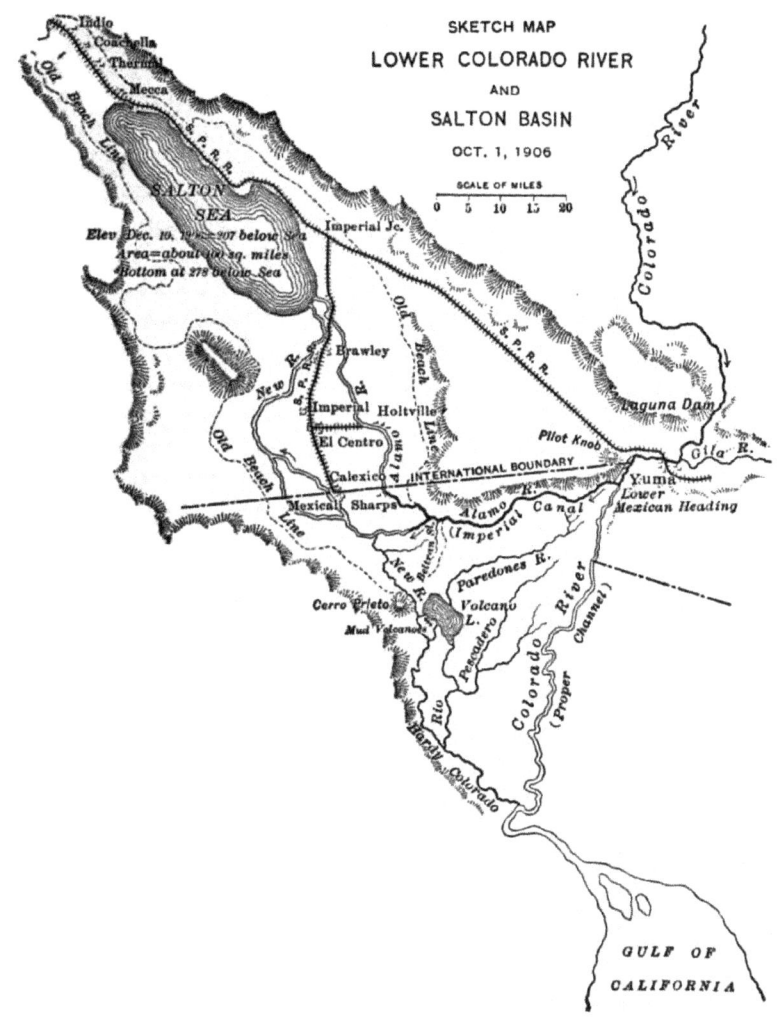

Fig. 64.

New River Cutting its Channel, Calexico 1906.

Fig. 65. The New River cataracts were about 1500 feet wide and 40-60 high, cutting back (from the Salton Sea traveling upstream) at approximately a third of a mile a day.

Fig. 66. The Beltran Slough in Mexico was one of the main links for water in the Alamo channel to reach the New River.

Fig. 67. An irrigation flume built over the New River.

Fig. 68. Wreck of flume to Irrigation District No. 8, Summer of 1905 (fallen debris can be seen in the right one-fourth of the photo, extending from ground level into the gorge).

Fig. 69. Overflow near Five Headings, June 1905.

Fig. 70. Homestead flooded near Five Headings.

Fig. 71. Residents of the Five Headings area cooling off in the summer heat, 1905.

Fig. 72. New River near town of Imperial, summer 1905.

Fig. 73. Another view of the New River near Imperial, summer 1905.

Fig. 74. New River northwest of Imperial, summer 1905. Banks collapsing can be seen in the right half of the photo.

Fig. 75. New River near Imperial.

Fig. 76. New River 4 miles northeast of Brawley, August 6, 1906. The "bucket" leaving from the far bank was used by people to cross the gorge via a cable strung over it.

181

CALEXICO AND MEXICALI

As the New River approached the Border, its cataracts threatened to undercut all in its path. The *Imperial Valley Press*[62] reported on July 7, 1906, the downtown of Mexicali had been washed away, leaving about 15 houses. Calexico appeared to be safer due to dynamiting the river to alter its course and construction of a 4 mile levee under the direction of C.N. Perry.

---

[62] *Imperial Valley Press*, Vol. No. 13, July 7, 1906, Front Page.

Fig. 77. Mexicali devastation by the New River, September 1, 1906.

Fig. 78. Looking downstream from Mexicali, September 1, 1906.

Fig. 79. Another view looking downstream from Mexicali, summer 1906.

Fig. 80. Ferry in New River gorge near Calexico, summer 1906.

Fig. 81. Border monument near Calexico.

Fig. 82. New River near Calexico. Ultimately the railway tracks were undercut and had to be moved.

Fig. 83. In a partially successful attempt to cut a channel away from Calexico, the New River was dynamited, June 14, 1906.

Fig. 84. Calexico was partially protected by a dike erected under the supervision of C.N. Perry, June 1906.

Fig. 85. View from temporary dike as the water spread out 10 miles wide at Calexico.

SOUTHERN PACIFIC RAILROAD

In July 1905, rising water in the new sea reached the railway tracks. To be able to continue operations on the main line from Los Angeles to New Orleans, the railway constructed shooflies (Fig. 88).[63] Number 11, built in February/March 1906, was 39 miles long. At the time it was built, it was estimated that it would enable rail travel for at least two years, but by October the water was 47.5 inches higher than when the shoofly was surveyed, and parts of the tracks were in trouble.

As shown on the map in Fig. 88, another shoofly (Number 12) was surveyed in early 1907, but only 4 miles of track had been laid from Mecca when the second closing succeeded.

Further south, the branch line from Imperial Junction to Calexico also had problems. The bridge north of Brawley had to be moved and extended five times; by 1915, it was 2,706 feet long. The crossing of the New River required three shooflies and eventually was 9,086 feet long.

The Inter-California Railroad, an extension of SP service into Mexico, had to be totally rebuilt through Calexico and Mexicali, as well as further south. As it approached the Colorado River, it was rerouted onto the new spur levee.

---

[63] Railway shooflies are usually temporary tracks laid to reroute the trains around an obstacle. Number 11, with improvements, became the permanent route by the Sea.

Fig. 86. Southern Pacific tracks being undercut near Calexico, September 1, 1906.

205

Fig. 87. The Salton Sea encroaching on the Southern Pacific tracks near Salton, 1905.

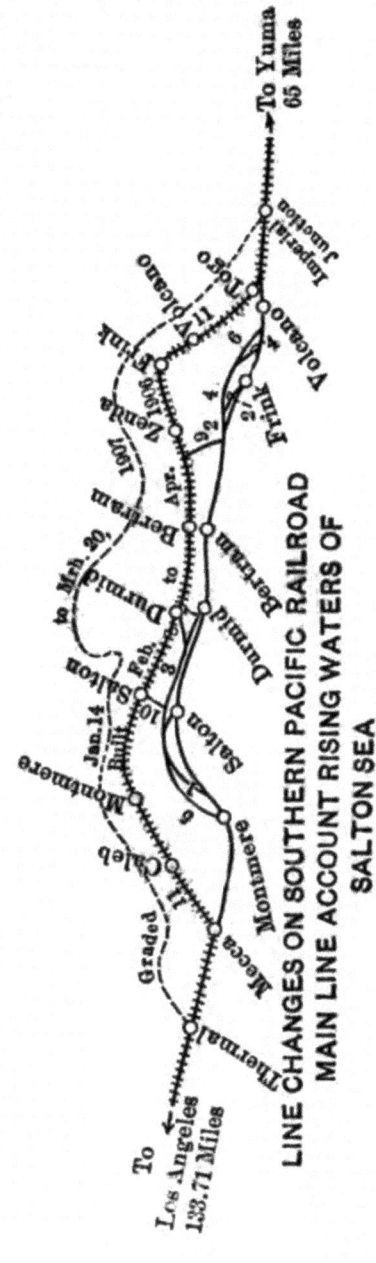

Fig. 88. Diagrams of main line and shooflies.

Fig. 89. Southern Pacific train on Salt Creek shoofly southeast of Salton, August 9, 1906.

Fig. 90. Shoofly about a mile southeast of Durmid, May 16, 1907.

Fig. 91. Salton Sea bay near Durmid, May 16, 1907.

Fig. 92. Salton Sea 2-3 miles from where the New River enters the Sea, May 15, 1907.

Fig. 93.—Bridge over Salton Sea—S. P. R. R. California–Arizona Route

Fig. 94.

NEW LIVERPOOL SALT WORKS

In the 1880s, George Durbrow and other investors had formed the New Liverpool Salt Works[64] at Salton, on the SP main line in the Coachella Valley. Salt was deposited on approximately 1000 acres of dry sea bed by seepage from salt springs. Although called a mine, the salt works actually resembled a harvest operation, needing only to cut salt from the field, crush it, bag it, and send it by narrow gauge rail to the nearby Southern Pacific station at Salton.

The quality, quantity, and uniqueness of its gathering led to it being featured in an 1899 issue of *Strand Magazine*[65] and a 1901 issue of the *National Geographic Magazine*.[66] *The Saline Deposits of California* described the operation:

> The sight at the salt works is an interesting one, for thousands of tons are piled up like huge snow drifts,...The Indians operate cable plows, harvesting over 700 tons of pure salt per day. A portable railroad conveys the salt to the works.
>
> The [crystal] lake is constantly being supplied by numerous springs in the adjacent foothills, which flow into

---

[64] Incorporated November 12, 1883, per Certified copy of Certificate of Incorporation attached to *California Development Company v New Liverpool Salt Company*, 97 C.C.A. 242, 172 Fed. 820 (1909), Complainant's Exhibit K.

[65] John R. Watkins, "A Common Crystal," *Strand Magazine*, Vol. XVII, No. 98 (London, 1899).

[66] Charles F. Holder, "A Remarkable Salt Deposit," *National Geographic Magazine*, Vol. XII, No. 11 (Washington, 1901).

the basin and quickly evaporate, leaving deposits of very pure salt that vary from 10 to 20 inches in thickness.[67]

Past overflows of the Colorado River were not unheard of, but had not been as disastrous. In February 1891, the Colorado overflowed its banks, into the Mexican delta, leaving water standing in low areas. The following June, it overflowed again, reaching the standing water; the resulting flood from the commingled waters reached the Salton Basin, creating a lake approximately 30 miles long and 10 miles wide, but only 5 feet deep. Being shallow, it evaporated, leaving the Salt Works intact.

In 1905, as the sea water rose, the salt field was submerged, then the salt plant, and then the town of Salton and the rail lines.[68]

The salt works were a total loss;[69] they still lie beneath the sea.

---

[67] Gilbert E. Bailey, "The Saline Deposits of California," *California State Mining Bureau,* Bulletin No. 24, (San Francisco, 1902), p. 124.

[68] According to the *Brotherhood of Locomotive Firemen's Magazine* (January, 1906), by Nov. 11, 1905, every building in Salton was surrounded by water except the depot, which was within 6 feet of the flood waters. Preparations were under way to move the depot 150 feet; eventually, the Salton Depot was moved to higher ground 3 times. Today, there is a metal equipment shed at Salton, on a "wide spot in the road" next to the train track, nothing more.

[69] *California Development Company v New Liverpool Salt Company*; on appeal, the Judgment for the Plaintiff (New Liverpool Salt Co.) was affirmed.

Fig. 95. A salt plow in operation at New Liverpool Salt Works, Salton, circa 1899.

Fig. 96. Salt at Salton salt works.

Fig. 97. Southern Pacific tracks near Salton in 1905, elevation 205 feet below sea level.

Fig. 98. Salton Station on the Southern Pacific, August 29, 1905.

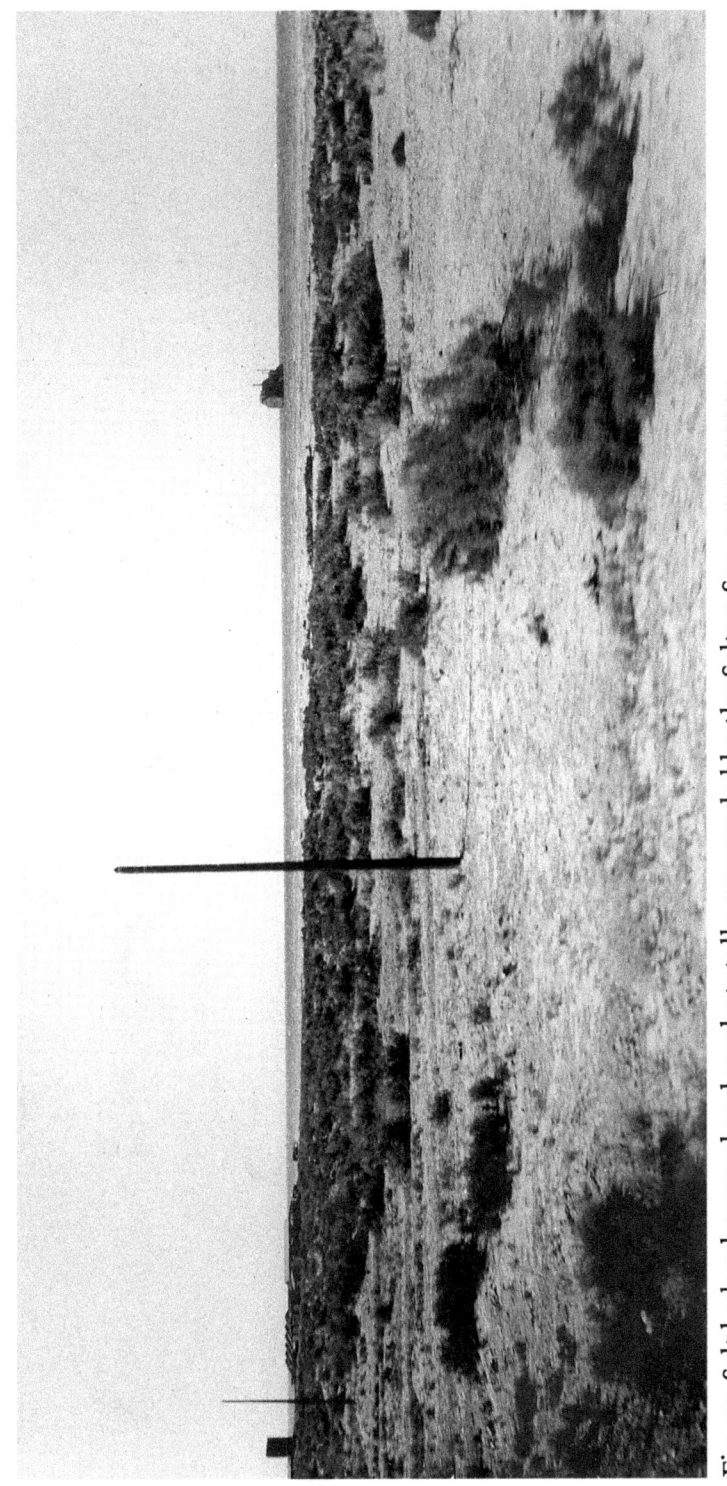

Fig. 99. Salt beds submerged and works totally surrounded by the Salton Sea, summer 1905.

Fig. 100. Southern Pacific tracks at Salton, August 29, 1905.

235

CONSEQUENCES FOR THE CAHUILLA

Many of the workers at the New Liverpool Salt Works were Native Americans, who lost their employment when the works flooded. They were not the only Cahuilla People to suffer loss.

On October 7, 1906, the *San Bernardino Daily Sun* reported Capt. Juaneta Razon, known as Fig Tree John,[70] visited Attorney John Brown Jr. of San Bernardino, to ask for help, describing the conditions at the northern end of the Sea:

> "Our houses are under water, the ground we tilled is the home of the fishes, our little ponies have to seek the hills for the bunch grass, and our women and children lie out under the stars, with no shelter over them but their blankets,..."[71]

The newspaper went on to state the Indians had a "large tract under cultivation," including plots of vegetables and alfalfa.

On October 9, 1906, Indian Agent L.A. Wright countered in an article that the only "red skins" who lost their homes were Fig Tree John and his brother, and that "he can at once take up lands anywhere in the reservation or near the villages and establish a new home just as good as the

---

[70] Various accounts state his name was spelled Juanita, Juanito, and Juan. However, he is remembered in the Coachella Valley by the name Fig Tree John (or Figtree John). His home was at Fig Tree John Springs, as shown on Government maps of the era.

[71] "Floods Cover Homes of Indians: Great Salt Sea Where Once the Red Men Tilled Soil," *San Bernardino Daily Sun*, Vol. 26, No. 51, 7 Oct. 1906, p. 10.

former one, if he wishes." [72]

However, there are many contemporary reports that Fig Tree John had a permanent home and an established plantation of fig trees at Fig Tree John Springs.[73] At the height of the flooding in 1907, the site of his original home was five feet, or more, under water, so he had no choice, moving to Agua Dulce Spring to start over. It is believed that after the water receded enough, he regularly visited his old home site, but that he lived at Agua Dulce until his death in 1927.

The Torres and Martinez Reservations had been established by President Grant by Executive Order in May 1876, and were merged under The Relief of Mission Indians Act of 1891. At that time, the original 640 acres set aside was expanded by about 12,000 more acres. During the flooding of 1905-1907, approximately 2000 acres of the 1891 reservation lands were inundated. Under the mistaken belief that the Sea would evaporate, an additional 12,000 acres was added to the reservation in 1909, of which approximately 9000 acres were then underwater. There were also tribal and individual Cahuilla lands near the perimeter of the Sea that could not be irrigated due to lack of drainage.

Following two legal actions, a 1982 action brought by the United States on behalf of the tribe against Imperial Irrigation District and Coachella Valley Water District, and a 1991 suit by the Tribe, a settlement was negotiated among the parties, subject to Congressional approval. Approximately 40% of the 24,024 acre reservation continued to be submerged as of the adoption by Congress of the Torres-Martinez Desert Cahuilla Indians Claims Settlement Act in 2000.[74]

---

[72] "Indian Agent Says Razon Dreamed: Red Man is Enjoying Life in Salton Basin," *San Bernardino Daily Sun*, Vol. 26, No. 52, 9 Oct. 1906, Pt. 2, p. 3.

[73] Frances Anthony in "Below Sea-Level," *The Land of Sunshine*, Vol. XV, No. 1, July 1901, described him as "the distinguished owner of an orchard of fig trees."

Jocie Wallace in "On the Desert," *The Youth's Instructor*, Vol. LIII, No. 42, Oct. 17, 1905, reported he had 30 fig trees over 30 years old at that time, plus numerous young trees.

[74] 25 U.S.C. Sections 1778-1778h.

Fig. 101. Salton Sea from Fig Tree John Springs, October 1906.

Fig. 102. Agua Dulce, the "new" home of Fig tree John, 1918.

Fig. 103. Fig Tree John, his wife and grandchildren, October 1905.

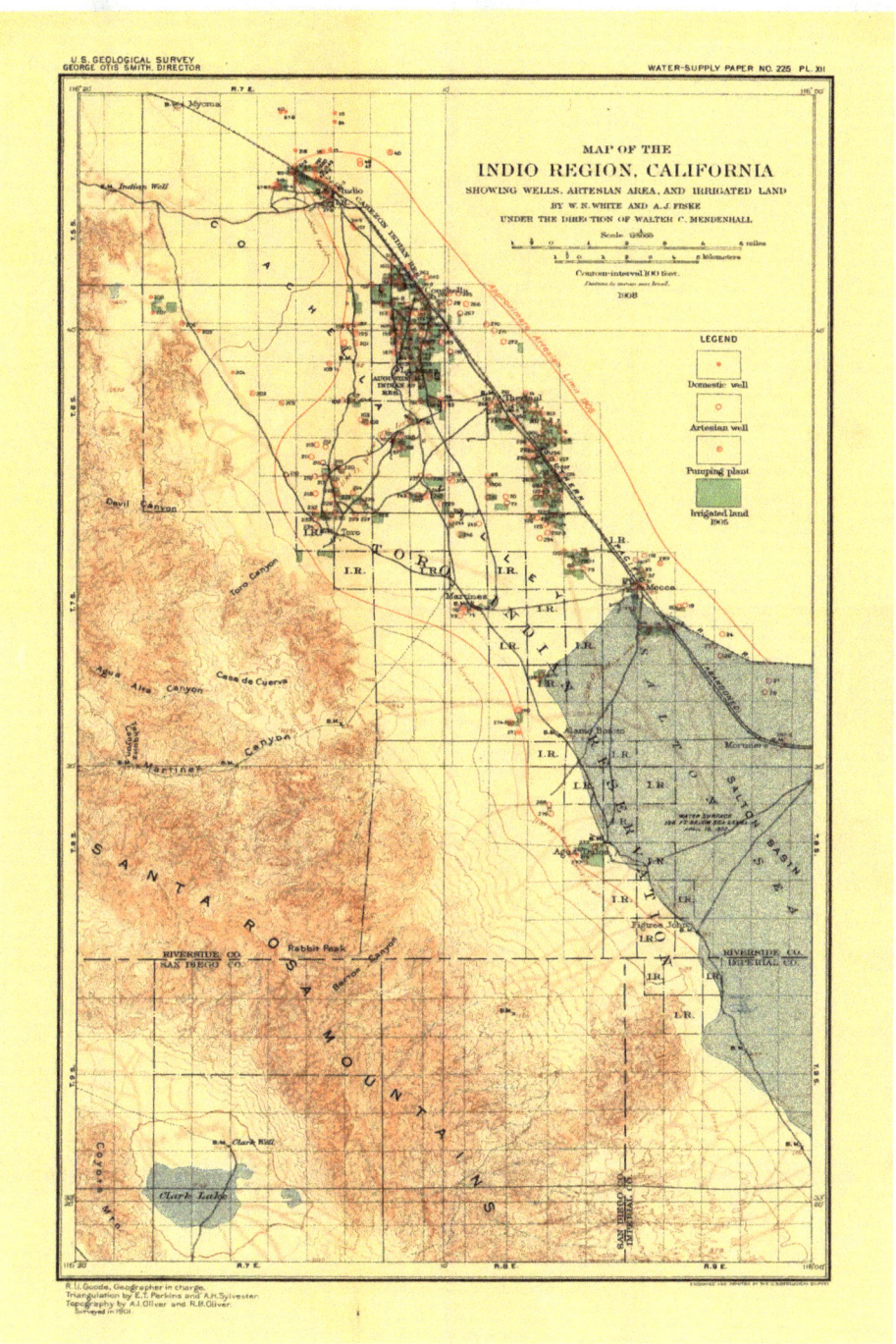

Fig. 104. 1908 USGS map, showing the "Toro" Indian Reservation and northern Salton Sea.

EPILOGUE

Charles Robinson Rockwood, after leaving CDC in 1906, moved to Los Angeles and then to the Santa Maria Valley. In 1914, he returned to the Imperial Valley and became General Manager of Imperial Irrigation District.

Anthony H. Heber died in a hotel fire in Goldfield, Nevada, in November 1906. His family continued to own ranch land in the Imperial Valley.

George Chaffey went on to develop irrigation and agriculture in the Owens Valley.[75]

Charles N. Perry became Imperial County Surveyor, and in 1918, General Manager of Imperial Irrigation District, succeeding C.K. Clarke.

Thomas J. Hind, Superintendent for the Hind Dam and the levees, became Superintendent of the East Coast Oil Company, a subsidiary of the SP, headquartered in Tampico, Mexico.

Clarence K. Clarke was active in restoring the Imperial Valley canal system following the closing of the breaks; in 1909, he became Superintendent of the Number One Irrigation District and later Assistant General Manager of the CDC under its Receiver. In 1916, he became General Manager and Chief Engineer of Imperial Irrigation District.

Harry Thomas Cory became a consulting engineer, based in San Francisco. In 1920, he was appointed to the Nile Commission by the British government.

Epes Randolph became president of the Southern Pacific Railroad of Mexico and Arizona Eastern Railway, and a member of the University of

---

[75] The project at Manzanar was successful until the City of Los Angeles, via the Los Angeles Aqueduct, drained the surface and groundwater from the area. Ultimately, the land was sold to the City, which leased it to the US Army for the site of the Japanese internment camp during World War II.

Arizona Board of Regents.

Edward Henry ("Ned") Harriman: to quote a story from George Kennan's book:

> Shortly before his death,[76] Mr. Harriman made a trip through the Imperial Valley and over the reconstructed levee which kept the Colorado River in bounds. Upon his return to Imperial Junction, he was met by a representative of the *Los Angeles Examiner* who, in conversation about the work, said:
>
> "Mr. Harriman, the government hasn't paid you that money, and your work here does not seem to be duly appreciated, do you not, under the circumstances, regret having made this large expenditure?"
>
> "No," replied Mr. Harriman. "This valley was worth saving, wasn't it?"
>
> "Yes," said the reporter.
>
> "Then we have the satisfaction of knowing we saved it, haven't we?"[77]

The story may be apocryphal, but I hope he felt that way. Yes, he was a titan of railroading, but also a humanitarian. The actions Harriman and the Southern Pacific Railroad took in rendering service during the San Francisco earthquake and fire disaster saved hundreds, if not thousands, of lives. In advancing funds, as well as engineers, equipment, materials, work trains, etc., to avert a total disaster in the Imperial, Mexicali, and lower Coachella Valleys, the Southern Pacific saved homes, farms, and towns. Railway tracks could have been rerouted at far less cost.

---

[76] 1909

[77] George Kennan, *The Salton Sea: An Account of Harriman's Fight with the Colorado River* (New York, The Macmillan Company, 1917), p. 105.

Fig. 105.

Fig. 106. The Salton Sea, circa 1920. From a souvenir book commissioned by the Southern Pacific for its passengers on *The Sunset Route*.

APPENDIX
SITES IN THE TWENTY-FIRST CENTURY

1. THE SALTON TROUGH from space, 2013; the mountains and Algodones Dunes are clearly seen between the river and the Imperial Valley. NASA photograph.

2. THE COLORADO above Imperial Dam, no longer a free river.

3. THE COLORADO as it exits Imperial Dam sluice gates into its old channel, on its way to Laguna Dam and Mexico.

4. LAGUNA DAM (1909) now regulates the sluiceway through the main channel of the Colorado, sending the water to Mexico.

5. PILOT KNOB FROM THE NORTHWEST. The Imperial Canal began at the east end of the rock (left end in this photo).

6. ARAZ JUNCTION. The spur going south is gone, but the main line still passes through.

7. PILOT KNOB area, March 2014. NASA photograph (some labels added).

8. ALL AMERICAN CANAL, near Hanlon Headgate, on its journey from Imperial Dam to the Imperial and Coachella Valleys.

9. HANLON HEADING, December 2017.

10. HANLON HEADGATE, December 2017.

11. Train tracks atop HANLON HEADGATE, December 2017, with machinery to lift gate for launch access on the left.

12. The ALAMO CANAL, December 2017. All that remains is a stretch between the 1918 Rockwood gate and a few hundred feet into Mexico.

13. PILOT KNOB at Hanlon. Quarrying is evident.

14. ALGODONES DUNES, between the Colorado River and the Imperial Valley, January 2018.

15. The ALAMO RIVER, south of Calipatria, March 2018. The gorge is wide and has eroded further at the river; this photograph was taken while standing about half way down from the level of the surrounding countryside.

16. This photograph was also taken in the ALAMO RIVER GORGE, about 200 feet from the river's current channel as seen in 15. At this location, the gorge is about 2000 feet across.

17. NEW RIVER, northwest of Imperial, January 2018.

18. NEW RIVER near Imperial, after 110 years, erosion is slowly remaking the gorge.

19. ALAMO RIVER entering the Salton Sea, April 2001. U.S. Bureau of Reclamation photograph.

20. NEW RIVER entering the Salton Sea, January 2005. U.S. Bureau of Reclamation photograph.

21. SALT CREEK, January 2001, U.S. Bureau of Reclamation photograph.

22. SALT CREEK TRESTLE, December 2017, near the site of Salton Station.

23. Site of the SALTON STATION, March 2018.

24. 2002 FIESTA at Martinez celebrating the settlement of the litigation over flooding of reservation lands.

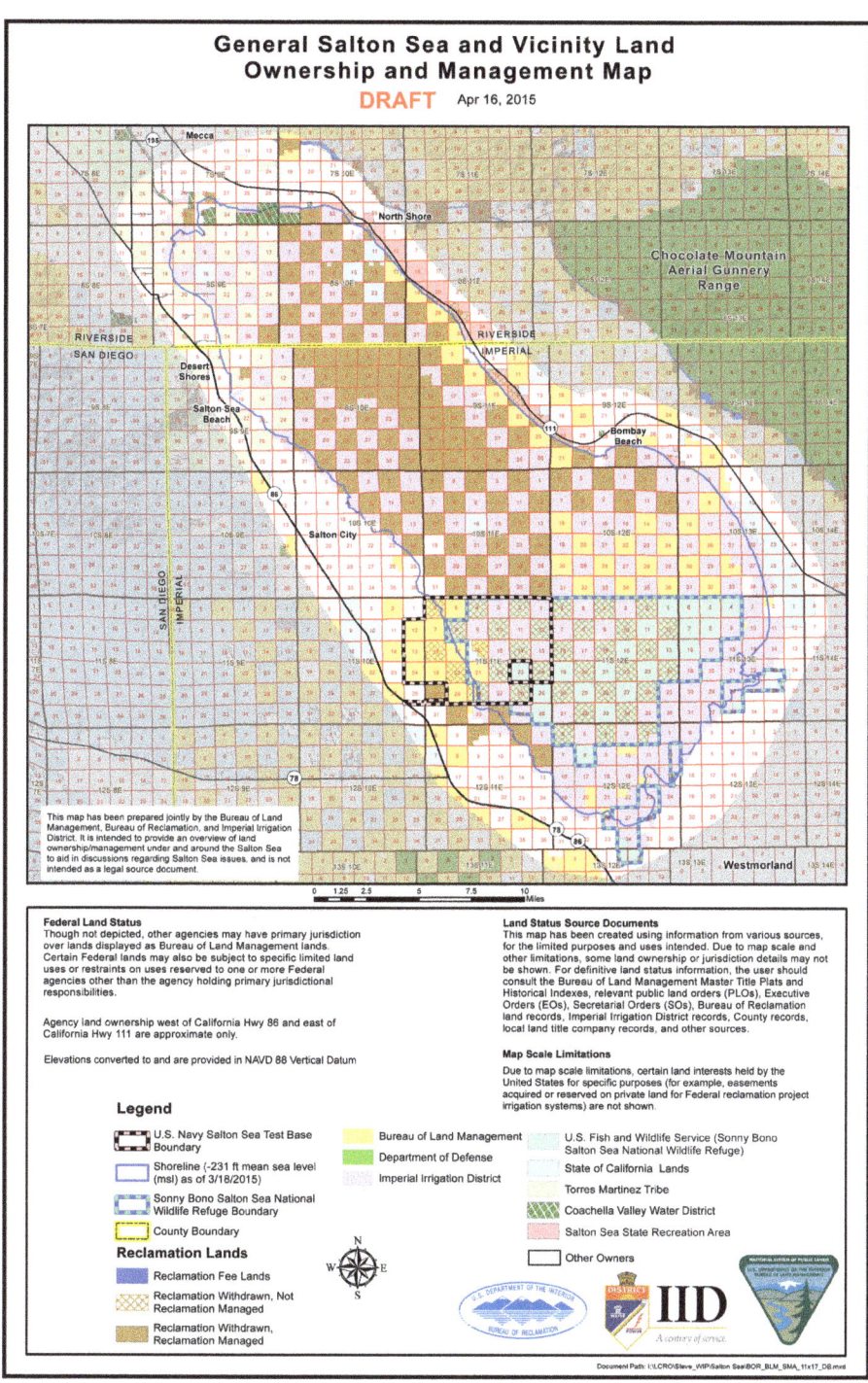

25. 2015 map showing flooded TORRES-MARTINEZ RESERVATION LAND.

26. MARCH 2018.

ILLUSTRATIONS: SOURCES AND NOTES THEREON

Illustrations:

Fig. 1. Photo by the author.

Fig. 2. Published in *The Imperial Valley and the Salton Sink* by H.T. Cory and W.P. Blake, 1915.

Fig. 3. Published in Cory & Blake.

Fig. 4. Promotional material by Imperial Land Company, circa 1904.

Fig. 5. Published in "The Innundation of the Salton Basin by the Colorado River and How It was Caused" by Allen Day, *Scientific American*, 1906, and in *The Story of the First Decade in Imperial Valley* by Edgar F. Howe and Wilbur Jay Hall, 1910.

Fig. 6. Published in Cory & Blake.

Fig. 7. Southern Pacific Company photo; published as a postcard by M. Rieder, Los Angeles, CA, circa 1912; used by The California Promotion Committee in various promotional materials prior to 1910.

Fig. 8. US Bureau of Reclamation photo (USBR); published in *The Lower Colorado River & the Salton Basin* by C.E. Grunsky, 1907.

Fig. 9. USBR photo.

Fig. 10. Published in "Transcript of Record," US Circuit Court of Appeals, for the Ninth Circuit. *The California Development Co., Appellant vs. New Liverpool Salt Co., Appellee*, 14 May 1908 (Case 1584); and in *The Salton Sea: An Account of Harriman's Fight with The Colorado River* by George Kennan, 1917.

Fig. 11. USBR photo.

Fig. 12. By L.C. Easton, Army Corp of Engineers, 1900 (US National Archives & Records Administration).

Fig. 13. USBR photo.

Fig. 14. US Geological Survey photo (USGS).

Fig. 15. Published in Case 1584 and Kennan.

Fig. 16. Published in "The Overflow" by George Wharton James,

Scientific American, 1906. Also, can be found: Courtesy of University of Southern California and the California Historical Society (USC/CHS, see Note 3 below).

Fig. 17. Published in *The Wonders of the Colorado Desert* by George Wharton James, 1906, (Note 5 below).

Fig. 18. Published in Cory & Blake.

Fig. 19. USBR photo.

Fig. 20. USGS photo.

Fig. 21. USBR photo.

Fig. 22. Published in Case 1584 and Kennan.

Fig. 23. USBR photo.

Fig. 24. Published in Case 1584 and Kennan.

Fig. 25. USBR photo; published in Grunsky and Case 1584.

Fig. 26. Published in Cory & Blake.

Fig. 27. USBR photo; published in Grunsky; Howe & Hall; and "The Salton Sea" by F.H. Newell, *Annual Report Smithsonian Institution,* 1907.

Fig. 28. USBR photo; published in Grunsky, and "The New Inland Sea" by Arthur P. Davis, *National Geographic,* 1907.

Fig. 29. USBR photo.

Fig. 30. USBR photo; published in Grunsky.

Fig. 31. USGS photo.

Fig. 32. Published in "Born of the Desert" by C.R. Rockwood, *The Calexico Chronicle,* 1909.

Fig. 33. Published in *Engineering News*, 1907, and in Cory & Blake.

Fig. 34. USGS photo.

Fig. 35. Published in *Railway Age*, 1907.

Fig. 36. USGS photo.

Fig. 37. USBR photo; published in Case 1584.

Fig. 38. USBR photo.

Fig. 39. USBR photo.

Fig. 40. Published in Case 1584 and Kennan.

Fig. 41. Published in "The Colorado River Closing" by W.D.H. Washington, *Scientific American,* 1907 and Case 1584.

Fig. 42. Published in Cory & Blake.

Fig. 43. USGS photo.

Fig. 44. USGS photo.

Fig. 45. Published in *Engineering News,* 1906.

Fig. 46. Published in Case 1584 and Kennan.

Fig. 47. USGS photo; published in "The Colorado Desert" by W.C. Mendenhall, *National Geographic,* 1909.

Fig. 48. USGS photo.

Fig. 49. USBR photo.

Fig. 50. Courtesy of USC/CHS. Their notes attribute this photo to G. W. James (Note 5).

Fig. 51. Published in Cory & Blake.

Fig. 52. USBR photo.

Fig. 53. USBR photo.

Fig. 54. Courtesy of USC/CHS. Their notes attribute this photo to C.C. Pierce (Note 5).

Fig. 55. USBR photo.

Fig. 56. USGS photo.

Fig. 57. Published in "Imperial Valley, California: Its Problems & Possibilities" by C.E. Tait, US Senate Doc. 246, 1908.

Fig. 58. USGS photo.

Fig. 59. Postcard published circa 1920. This appears to have been printed by Curt Teich Co. 1898-1978, under the CT American Art Colored name. Although there is no letter prefix, from the production number, #105159, it was produced between 1908 & 1928. The Rockwood headgate was not built until 1918, narrowing this to 1918-1928. No copyright symbol.

Fig. 60. Postcard from USBR photo.

Fig. 61. Published in "A Representative Western Artist" by George Wharton James, *The Twentieth Century Magazine* (1910). Photo credit to G.W. James (Note 5).

Fig. 62. Published in *Wonders of the Colorado Desert* by George Wharton James, 1906. Photo credit to G.W. James (Note 5).

Fig. 63. Courtesy of USC/CHS. Their notes attribute this photo to C.C. Pierce (Note 5).

Fig. 64. Published in Grunsky.

Fig. 65. USBR photo; published in many articles and reports on the flooding; Case 1584; and as a postcard as seen here.

Fig. 66. Published in Case 1584.

Fig. 67. Courtesy of USC/CHS, circa 1907.

Fig. 68. USGS photo.

Fig. 69. USGS photo.

Fig. 70. USGS photo; published in Water-Supply Paper 225, 1909.

Fig. 71. USGS photo.

Fig. 72. USGS photo.

Fig. 73. USGS photo.

Fig. 74. USGS photo; published in Water-Supply Paper 225.

Fig. 75. USGS photo.

Fig. 76. USBR photo; published in Grunsky.

Fig. 77. USGS photo; published in Davis, Grunsky, Howe & Hall, and Case 1584.

Fig. 78. USGS photo.

Fig. 79. USGS photo.

Fig. 80. USGS photo.

Fig. 81. Courtesy of USC/CHS.

Fig. 82. Courtesy of USC/CHS.

Fig. 83. Published in *Out West* 1906 (photo credit to C.K. Smith) and *Railway Age* 1907 (photo credit to J.E. Peak). Could this be another example of photos being sold?

Fig. 84. Published in *Scientific American* 1907; Cory & Blake; and "A History of Calexico" by Margaret Romer. *Annual Publication of the Historical Society of Southern California* 1922.

Fig. 85. Published in *Out West* 1906 and *Smithsonian Annual Report*, 1907.

Fig. 86. USBR photo. Published in Davis; *Railroad Gazette* 1907; *Scientific American*; and "The Diversion of the Colorado River into the Salton Sea and the Efforts Made to Restore It to Its Former Channel" by J.A. Ockerson, *The Journal of the Association of Engineering Societies* 1907.

Fig. 87. USGS photo. Published in Howe & Hall.

Fig. 88. Published in Cory & Blake.

Fig. 89. USBR photo.

Fig. 90. USBR photo; published in Davis; *Railroad Gazette*; and Ockerson.

Fig. 91. USGS photo.

Fig. 92. USGS photo.

Fig. 93. Postcard; published by Newman Post Card Company, Los Angeles, San Francisco; message on back is dated 9-26-1910.

Fig. 94. Postcard, circa 1909; published by Newman Post Card Company, Los Angeles, San Francisco.

Fig. 95. Published in "A Common Crystal" by John R. Watkins, *Strand Magazine* 1899; and "The Saline Deposits of California" by Gilbert E. Bailey, *California State Mining Bureau*, Bulletin 24, 1902.

Fig. 96. Published in "A Remarkable Salt Deposit" by Charles F. Holder, *Scientific American* 1901, and reprinted in National Geographic 1901; reprinted as a postcard with no publisher given.

Fig. 97. USGS photo.

Fig. 98. USBR photo.

Fig. 99. USGS photo.

Fig. 100. Published in Davis; *Railroad Gazette*; *Scientific American 1907*; and Ockerson.

Fig. 101. USGS photo.

Fig. 102. Published in *California Desert Trails*, by J. Smeaton Chase, 1919.

Fig. 103. Published in "On the Desert," *The Youth's Instructor*, by Jocie Wallace, 1905.

Fig. 104. USGS map.

Fig. 105. Postcard, published by BNCo, prior to 1922.

Fig. 106. Published in *The Sunset Route: El Paso to Los Angeles*, a souvenir book by Van Noy-Interstate Co., Curt Teich & Co. 1921 (2 pages, no numbers assigned).

Appendix of Modern Photos and Map of the Sea:

No. 1. NASA, 2013

Nos. 2-6, 8-18, 22-24, and 26 the author

No. 7. NASA, 2014; some labels have been added

No. 19 & 21. USBR, 2001

No. 20. USBR, 2005

No. 25. USBR, Imperial Irrigation District, Bureau of Indian Affairs map, 2015.

NOTES on US Copyright:

1) Photographs and maps by federal government employees, created in the course of their employment, are in the Public Domain. This applies to United States Geological Survey (USGS), United States Bureau of Reclamation (USBR), the Army Corp of Engineers, Bureau of Indian Affairs, and NASA.

From its organization in July 1902, until March 9, 1907, the US Reclamation Service (later to be known as the US Bureau of Reclamation) was a part of the USGS; photographs from this period may bear either designation, or in some instances are found in both archives.

2) Works published in the U.S. prior to 1923 are in the Public Domain.

3) Copyright notice for images from USC/CHS: Public Domain. Release under the CC BY Attribution license — http://creativecommons.org/licenses/by/3.0/ — Credit both "University of Southern California. Libraries" and "California Historical Society."

4) In *Bridgeman Art Library, Ltd. v. Corel Corp.*, 36 F. Supp. 2d 191 (S.D.N.Y. 1999), U.S. District Court Judge Kaplan found mere mechanical reproduction of an image does not make that image subject to copyright. I agree with those who believe this principle would be applied to digitally scanned images also, and to standardized Photoshop restoration. Therefore, I claim no copyright to any of the old photos in this book. I do reserve all rights to my modern photographs (attributed to "the author" above).

I have digitally manipulated many, if not all, of the old photos in this book, changing sizes, resolution, removing "noise," altering "lighting" etc. But, I have not altered the images by adding content, except Fig. 48, to which

I added a "pencil line" to mark the break in the levee, and to Modern Photo No. 7, to which I added labels, as noted in their captions.

5) Photos attributed to George Wharton James and C.C. Pierce are problematic; according to The Huntington Library: "Aside from making his own photographs, Pierce acquired the negatives and prints of other regional photographers such as Emil Ellis, Parker and Knight, Ramsey, Herve Friend, L.M. Clendenon, George P. Thresher, George Wharton James, and F.M. Huddleston. Pierce eradicated the existing signatures from the photographs, stamped his own name on the images, and organized the lot into subject files. The consequence of Pierce's business practices assured that most, if not all, of the connections between the images and their original creator are now lost. However, the archive which he advertised as the 'C.C. Pierce Collection of Rare, Historical and Curious Photographs, Illustrating California, the Pacific Coast and the Southwest,' became an invaluable resource for researchers and boosters alike, all of whom came to Pierce's shop to locate an image for their purposes."
(http://www.oac.cdlib.org/findaid/ark:/13030/kt7199q9m3/)

I assume he either purchased the copyrights, or the early photographers accepted the practice, as he extensively advertised this collection and I can find no litigation for infringement.

Posterity is indebted to him for preserving the images.

BIBLIOGRAPHY

1906 Annual Report of the Southern Pacific Company.

1907 Annual Report of the Southern Pacific Company.

1930 Annual Report of the Southern Pacific Company.

Anthony, Frances. "Below Sea-Level." *The Land of Sunshine*, vol. XV, no. 1, 7 July 1901, pp. 22-26.

Bailey, Gilbert E. "The Saline Deposits of California." *California State Mining Bureau*, Bulletin 24, May 1902.

Byers, Charles Alma. "The Possibilities of the Salton Sea." *The Popular Science Monthly*, Jan. 1907.

Chase, J. Smeaton. *California Desert Trails.* Houghton Mifflin Co., 1919.

"Closing the Break of the Colorado River into the Salton Sea." *Railroad Gazette*, 15 Feb. 1907, pp. 217-220.

"Colorado River Crevasse and Salton Sea - The Great Work of Control." *The Railway Age,* vol. 42, no. 18, 2 Nov. 1906, pp. 547-548.

"Controlling the Colorado River and Salton Sea." *Scientific American,* vol. 95, no. 25, 22 Dec. 1906, pp. 467-469.

Cory, H. T. "Closing the Break of the Colorado River Into the Salton Sink." *Engineering News*, vol. 56, no. 26, 27 Dec. 1906, pp. 671-674.

Cory, H. T. "Closing the New Break in the Colorado River." *The Engineering Record Building Record, and Sanitary Engineer*, vol. 55, no. 9, 2 Mar. 1907, pp. 293-295.

Cory, H. T. "Colorado River Crevasse and Salton Sea." *The Railway Age*, vol. 43, no. 24, 14 June 1907, pp. 953-958.

Cory, Harry Thomas, and William Phipps Blake. *The Imperial Valley and The Salton Sink.* John J. Newbegin, 1915.

Cory, H. T. "Report on the Financial Condition of the California Development Company and Its Subsidiary Company, La Sociedad de Riego y Terrenos de la Baja California, S.A." A report prepared for the Southern Pacific Company, 1 Nov. 1906.

Davis, Arthur P. "The New Inland Sea." *National Geographic*, vol. 18, no.1, Jan. 1907, pp. 37–48.

Day, Allen. "The Innundation of the Salton Basin by the Colorado River and How It was Caused." *Scientific American*, vol. 94, no. 15, 14 April 1906, pp. 310-312.

"Destruction of Mexicali Well Nigh Complete. Calexico Apparently Safe." *The Imperial Valley Press*, vol. 6, no. 13, Saturday, 7 July 1906, p. 4.

Duryea, Edwin, Jr. "The Salton Sea Menace." *Out West*, vol. 24, no. 1, Jan. 1906, pp. 3-24.

Duryea, Edwin, Jr. "The Salton Sink Problem." *Engineering News*, vol. 55, no. 11, May 1906, p. 300.

Farr, F. C., editor. *Imperial Valley, California*. Elms & Franks, 1908.

"Floods Cover Homes of Indians: Great Salt Sea Where Once the Red Men Tilled Soil." *San Bernardino Daily Sun*, vol. 26, no. 51, Sunday, 7 Oct. 1906, p. 10.

"Government Aid Needed." *Los Angeles Herald*, vol. 34, no. 76, Sunday, 16 Dec. 1906, p. 20.

Grunsky, C. E. "The Lower Colorado and the Salton Basin." *American Society of Civil Engineers: Papers & Discussions*, vol. 33, no. 2, Feb. 1907, pp. 102–152.

Hall, Sharlot M. "The Problem of the Colorado River." *Out West*, vol. 25, no. 4, Oct. 1906, pp. 305–332.

Havens, F.G. "Why Public Ownership is Necessary." *The Imperial Press*, vol. 5, no. 7, Saturday, 3 June 1905, pp. 1 & 8.

Holder, Charles F. "A Remarkable Salt Deposit." *National Geographic*, vol. 12, no. 11, Nov. 1901, pp. 390–392.

Holt, L. M., compiler. *Unfriendly Attitude of the United States Government Towards the Imperial Valley*. Imperial Daily Standard Print, 1907.

Howe, Edgar F., and Wilbur Jay Hall. *The First Decade In Imperial Valley*. Edgar F. Howe & Sons, 1910.

"Imperial River," *The Imperial Press*, vol. 5, no. 7, Saturday, 3 June 1905, p. 4.

"Indian Agent Says Razon Dreamed: Red Man is Enjoying Life in Salton Basin." *San Bernardino Daily Sun*, vol. 26, No. 52, Tuesday, 9 Oct. 1906, Pt. 2, p. 3.

James, George Wharton. *California.* The Page Company, 1914.

James, George Wharton. "The Innundation of the Salton Basin by the Colorado River and How It was Caused." *Scientific American*, vol. 94, no. 16, 21 April 1906, pp. 328-329.

James, George Wharton. *The Wonders of the Colorado Desert.* vol. I & II, Little, Brown, and Company, 1906.

Kelly, Allen. "Imperial Valley Fully Protected." *Los Angeles Sunday Times*, Sunday, 30 June 1907, p. 4.

Kennan, George. *The Salton Sea: An Account of Harriman's Fight with The Colorado River.* The Macmillan Company, 1917.

LaRue, E.C. "Colorado River and Its Utilization." *US Geological Survey*, Water-Supply Paper 395, Government Printing Office, 1916.

"Latest From River: To Stockholders of Imperial Water Co. No. 5." *The Imperial Press*, vol. 5, no. 7, Saturday, 3 June 1905, p. 6.

Martin, Frank G. "The New Inland Sea in California." *Appleton's Booklovers Magazine*, vol. 7, no. 5, May 1906, pp. 679-684.

Mendenhall, Walter C. "Ground Waters of the Indio Region, California." *US Geological Survey*, Water-Supply Paper 225, Government Printing Office, 1909.

Mendenhall, W. C. "The Colorado Desert." *National Geographic*, vol. 20, no. 8, August 1909, pp. 681-701.

Newell, F. H. "The Salton Sea." *Annual Report Smithsonian Institution*, 1907, pp. 331-345.

"Notes on Closing the Break in the Colorado River." *Engineering News*, vol. 57, no. 8, 21 Feb. 1907, pp. 210-212.

Ockerson, J. A. "The Diversion of the Colorado River into the Salton Sea and the Efforts Made to Restore It to Its Former Channel." *The Journal of the Association of Engineering Societies*, vol. 38, no. 6, June 1907, pp. 261-271.

"President Roosevelt, and President Harriman of the Southern Pacific Co., on Closing the Colorado River Break." *Engineering News*, vol. 56, no. 26, 27 Dec. 1906, p. 675.

"Railroad Damages from Inundation." *Brotherhood of Locomotive Firemen's Magazine*, vol. 40, Indianapolis, January 1906, pp. 19-20

"Reported Help From Southern Pacific." *The Imperial Press*, vol. 5, no. 7, Saturday, 3 June 1905, p .9.

Rockwood, C. R. "Born of the Desert: Imperial Valley in Its Making: Not a Dream." *The Second Annual Magazine Edition, The Calexico Chronicle*, May 1909, pp. 10-28.

Rockwood, C. R. "In The Matter of the Liability of the California Development Company in the Flooding of the Salton Basin." Written report, no date.

Romer, Margaret. "A History of Calexico." *Annual Publication of the Historical Society of Southern California*, vol. 12, no. 2, 1922, pp. 26-66.

Rowley, William D. *The Bureau of Reclamation: Origins and Growth to 1945.* Vol. 1, Bureau of Reclamation, U.S. Dept. of the Interior, Government Printing Office, 2006.

"Salton Sea Has Reached Southern Pacific Tracks." *Los Angeles Herald*, vol. 32, no. 298, Wednesday, 26 July 1905, p. 1.

Schulyer, James D. "The Overflow of Colorado River into Salton Basin." Written report, 20 Mar. 1907.

Schulyer, James D. "The Reinforced Concrete, Steel Headgates for the Imperial Canal, Colorado River." *Engineering News*, vol. 56, no. 26, 27 Dec. 1906, p. 675.

Supreme Court of California. *Title Insurance & Trust vs. California Development Co.,* 171 Cal.173, 152P542 (1915).

Tait, C. E. *Irrigation in Imperial Valley, California: Its Problems and Possibilities.* United States Congress, Senate, 60th Congress, 1st Session, Document 246. Government Printing Office, 1908.

"The Coming Visit of the Irrigation Committees." *The Imperial Press*, vol. 5, no. 7, Saturday, 3 June 1905, p. 4.

The Sunset Route: El Paso to Los Angeles, a souvenir photo book by Van Noy-Interstate Co., Curt Teich & Co. 1921, fifteenth photo (no page numbers).

"The Water's Work: How It has Cut Large Channels Through Imperial Valley." *The Imperial Valley Press*, vol. 6, no. 13, Saturday, 7 July 1906, pp. 1-2.

"Tide is Rising in Salton Sea." *The Imperial Press*, vol. 5, no. 7, Saturday, 3 June 1905, p. 5.

US Circuit Court of Appeals, for the Ninth Circuit. *The California Development Co., Appellant vs. New Liverpool Salt Co., Appellee.* Transcript of Record, 7 volumes, filed 14 May 1908 (Case 1584).

United States Congress, House, Committee on Claims. "Southern Pacific Imperial Valley Claim." Government Printing Office, 1908. 60th Congress, 1st Session, transcript.

Wallace, Jocie. "On the Desert." *The Youth's Instructor*, vol. 53, no. 42, 17 Oct. 1905, p. 2.

Washington, W. D. H. "The Colorado River Closure." *Scientific American*, vol. 96, no. 18, 4 May 1907, pp. 374-377.

Watkins, John R.. "A Common Crystal." *Strand Magazine*, vol. 17, no. 98, Feb. 1899, pp. 174–175.

"Will Hurry Plan: Officers of Railroad and Development Company Meet and Consult." *The Imperial Valley Press*, vol. 6, no. 13, Saturday, 7 July 1906, p. 4.

"Working to Subdue Colorado River." *Railway World*, 12 Oct. 12, 1906, pp. 869-870.

This book is set in EB Garamond (by Georg Duffner), courtesy of fontsquirrel.com:

"EB Garamond is an open source project to create a revival of Claude Garamont's famous humanist typeface from the mid-16th century. Its design reproduces the original design by Claude Garamont: The source for the letterforms is a scan of a specimen known as the "Berner specimen", which, composed in 1592 by Conrad Berner, son-in-law of Christian Egenolff and his successor at the Egenolff print office, shows Garamont's roman and Granjon's italic fonts at different sizes. Hence the name of this project: Egenolff-Berner Garamond."
https://www.fontsquirrel.com/fonts/eb-garamond

The style of the book contents is intentionally similar to the style of early Twentieth Century books, i.e. footnotes at the bottom of the page, and photographs and maps reproduced full page, each on its own leaf, with the exception of the modern photographs and map.

Ellen Lloyd Trover's interest in water projects started early as her parents owned and operated a heavy earthwork construction firm specializing in federal, state and municipal water systems; she grew up in the Coachella Valley 15 miles from the Salton Sea, and has returned to live on the family farm. A graduate of Vassar College (history major) and the Marshall-Wythe School of Law at The College of William & Mary, now retired from the practice of law, she continues to be active as the California State Senate Appointee to the Governing Board of the Coachella Valley Mountains Conservancy, Vice President of the Riverside County Farm Bureau, and a Director of Coachella Valley Irrigated Lands Coalition.

Birth of the Inland Sea brings together her interests in history, the sea, and railroads. She has recently launched a website on lesser-known history in the Southwest at www.HistoryTrove.com.

www.ingramcontent.com/pod-product-compliance
Lightning Source LLC
Chambersburg PA
CBHW062108290426
44110CB00023B/2749